ISLAMIC TWO-HEADED BEAST

By

Will Clark

ISLAMIC TWO-HEADED BEAST

Copyright© 2015 by Will Clark

ISBN-13: 978-1511898195
ISBN-10: 1511898194

Published by
Motivation Basics
P.O. Box 6327
Diamondhead, MS 39525
Will01@aol.com

For more information visit the author at
AuthorsDen.com

QUOTE

"A nation can survive its fools, and even the ambitious. But it cannot survive treason from within. An enemy at the gates is less formidable, for he is known and carries his banner openly. But the traitor moves amongst those within the gate freely, his sly whispers rustling through all the alleys, heard in the very halls of government itself. For the traitor appears not a traitor; he speaks in accents familiar to his victims, and he wears their face and their arguments, he appeals to the baseness that lies deep in the hearts of all men. He rots the soul of a nation, he works secretly and unknown in the night to undermine the pillars of the city, he infects the body politic so that it can no longer resist. A murderer is less to fear. The traitor is the plague."

Marcus Tullius Cicero, 58 B.C. Speech in the Roman Senate

SNAKES

Would you stroll barefoot through snake-infested grass?

Only if you want those snakes to kill you.

Would you wait for an enemy to attack you before you
consider owning a weapon?

Only if you want that snake to kill you.

There are two kinds of snakes:

Snakes in the grass don't strike unless you disturb them.

That other snake seeks you out to destroy you;
He was first discovered in the Garden of Eden;
His name is Evil.

Revelation names his son the Beast.

HE VOWS TO KILL YOU.
YOU MUST BE ARMED
AND
PREPARED TO DEFEAT HIM.

Barack Hussein Obama
Always Wears Just One Ring
It's Engraved with Two Coiled Serpents
http://www.snopes.com/politics/obama/weddingring.asp

CONTENTS

Introduction

America is under attack by Muslims who plan to destroy our way of life. They say it; they repeat it; they throw those words and those ideas right in our faces. They aren't subtle; they aren't hinting; they are deadly serious. Why are our leaders responsible for the safety and survival of American citizens ignoring this clear and deadly threat? Are they ignorant; are they oblivious; are they ignoring the threat; or are they in some way part of a real conspiracy to destroy our great nation that offers hope and freedom for so many?

Perhaps our leaders are aware of one of those threats to destroy America and our way of life; that life of freedom and aspirations to become something even greater than the life and prosperity our Founding Fathers planned and hoped for us. They seem somewhat aware that we are being attacked by a vicious force; that force of radical Islamic extremism, which they label terrorism.

Terrorist attacks have happened in America, and the anticipation of more attacks keeps our security forces on high alert to thwart those that are detected. Visible Islamic extremism, terrorism, is only one head of the deadly snake, that ancient serpent that plans to destroy Godliness and freedom; especially in Israel and the United States. It's the serpent that says it will kill anyone who doesn't convert to what they call their 'religion of peace.' What's most amazing is that many people voluntarily convert into this system, this deadly cult that calls itself a 'religion.' Would the god of any religion demand non-believers be killed, even beheaded? Are Muslim leaders suggesting salvation can be achieved by force, intimidation, and murder? Shouldn't one seek eternal salvation through a calling into that religion - not by force? That forced salvation suggests an evil intent, perhaps led by an ancient serpent.

That serpent, that ancient dragon introduced in the Book of Genesis, has another head. Our danger is that two-headed serpent. One head guides blatant terrorism; while the other, the Muslim Brotherhood, is more surreptitious in its approach. The Muslim Brotherhood is attacking America, and plans to destroy us, while we watch only for the attack by that more active snake, terrorists. That two-headed serpent is playing a deadly game to destroy us. Our leaders, in their efforts to be politically correct, are helping that deceitful snake accomplish its goal.

While one head openly and directly attacks; the other head slithers evil into the quietest corners of our nation and our government. This evil one slithers so stealthily he beguiles those tasked to defend our nation against him. This head is the head of a 'woman,' a religion that 'sits upon a scarlet colored beast, full of names of blasphemy, having seven heads and ten horns.' Revelation 17:3. It's the same woman (religion) 'drunken with the blood of the saints, and with the blood of the martyrs of Jesus.' Revelation 17:6.

These Bible quotes identify only one possible religion that fits that description. That religion is Islam. The 'scarlet colored beast' is the one described as 'a deceiver and a blasphemer;' the beast of Revelation.

The purpose for this small book is to present enough pertinent information to further describe the dangers of this religion and this beast to the peace and tranquility of our nation and our world. If we understand this beast, where it came from, and his ulterior motives and plans, then perhaps we will know how to stop it and defeat it - even destroy it. And, to take the first step to do that, every competent American citizen must be armed. Yes, every citizen must be required to own a personal weapon. But, many people and many organizations and institutions try to discourage and even ban private ownership of personal firearms.

Perhaps before we discuss and interpret the two-headed evil, we should discuss personal weapons. Those charged most with our security and protection often are the ones most determined to confiscate our weapons of personal security. They imagine they are doing our nation a great service by eliminating those dangerous weapons from the hands of people who could become dangerous, and a hazard to society. In effect, those who confiscate weapons from competent private citizens are accommodating the slithering approach of that dangerous snake; the one slithering from within; the Muslim Brotherhood..

Islamic Two-Headed Beast   Will Clark

Chapter 1
Personal Weapons

In 1791, the Bill of Rights, including the Second Amendment, was ratified. It stated "A well regulated militia, being necessary to the security of a free state, the right of the people to keep and bear arms, shall not be infringed."

The first open attempt to ban personal firearms came in 1837. That year Georgia passed a law to ban handguns. The law was ruled unconstitutional and thrown out. Perhaps this was the beginning of the great gun debate; should private individuals be allowed to own firearms. Soon afterwards, other gun control actions were considered:

In reaction to emancipation, in 1865, some southern states passed laws which excluded newly-freed blacks from owning weapons.

The National Rifle Association (NRA) was formed in 1871having as it's main goal to improve civilian marksmanship in case of war.

Congress banned the sale of concealable firearms by mail, in1927.

The National Firearms Act of 1934 was passed regulating fully automatic firearms such as sub-machine guns which were popular by gangsters at that time.

The first limitation on the sale of regular firearms was by the Federal Firearms Act of 1938. Anyone who sold guns were required to purchase a Federal Firearms License and to maintain a record of names and addresses of purchasers. They were not allowed to sell guns to violent felons. The annual license fee was $1.

Perhaps serious gun control measures were not considered until President John F. Kennedy was assassinated in 1963. Until then, common weapons mostly for hunting and target shooting, such as shotguns, rifles, handguns, and ammunition were routinely sold over the counter and by mail-order to adults. The assassination sparked a deep debate about gun control.

Resulting from that deeper scrutiny of private weapons ownership, the Gun Control Act of 1968 was passed. The act was to limit sale of firearms to only those who were more qualified and responsible, and who were legally authorized. Criminal backgrounds, competency and drug involvement were listed as major considerations for gun purchase and ownership. It also increased the emphasis on licensing and records keeping of gun dealers, and other who sold guns.

There have also been many individual, local, and state actions to limit firearms or their sales. Four actions in 1998 represent common attacks:

In October, 1998, New Orleans filed a lawsuit against gun

dealers, manufacturers, and associations, and sought to recover costs related to gun violence.

In November 1998, Chicago filed a $433 million lawsuit against manufacturers and sellers, claiming that oversupplying guns contributed to increased costs caused by too many criminals with guns.

In November 1998, when a young California boy was killed by another boy with a Beretta pistol, the family brought suit against Beretta for being the gun maker. The suit was dismissed by a local Jury.

In December 1998, the National Rifle Association had to file a lawsuit to block collection of gun buyers' information by the FBI.

These are only representative examples of the many and continuing attacks on gun owners, dealers, and manufacturers to halt or discourage ownership of personal firearms. These attacks continue, and will likely increase as the federal government gains more executive power to control our daily lives. When will this encroaching unconstitutional power end? Most likely with the total ban against ownership of firearms. Although the Supreme Court has time and time again upheld the right of private citizens to own personal weapons, some parts of government find ways to deny citizens that right.

An article titled: 'Right to Bear Arms? Gun grabbing sweeping the nation' by Malia Zimmerman, published April 09, 2015 by FoxNews.com, gave a glaring example. The article begins:

"Cherished family heirlooms were among the 21 firearms Michael Roberts surrendered to the Torrance Police Department in 2010, after his doctor filed a restraining order against him.

The court order was the result of a dispute Roberts had with a member of the doctor's staff and, after Roberts pleaded no contest, the matter was resolved. Yet, even though he filed the proper Law Enforcement Gun Release paperwork on four separate occasions, obtained clearance from the California Department of Justice and had two court orders commanding the return of his guns, police refused to hand them over.

With the backing of the National Rifle Association and California Rifle and Pistol Association, Roberts filed a federal lawsuit in May 2014, over the $15,500 worth of firearms. In the end he got the money, but not the guns. The police had had them destroyed."

This is a common practice in many locations. Although he was compensated for the value of his guns; nevertheless, he was refused his Second Amendment right to own those weapons. Money does not take the place of the right to defend oneself. An attacker has never been shot and killed, or deterred, with a thicker wallet or purse.

A similar case took place in Glendale, Arizona, when a Navy veteran had a dispute with his neighbor about chemical odors coming from his neighbor's truck, frequently parked in front of his house. When the police got involved, they confiscated his entire collection of firearms, 28 in all, with a value of about $25,000. Even if his firearms are eventually returned, the cost of that process will likely be more than the value of the firearms, which is the case in most illegal firearm confiscation. Gun owners simply cannot afford the cost of the process to get their guns back.

"While Americans have the constitutional rights to keep and bear arms – and protect their property from government's unlawful seizure – it is not just in California where guns are seized and destroyed illegally, attorneys charge."

"This kind of below-the-radar bureaucratic gun confiscation is a growing Second Amendment and property rights violation problem, particularly in strict gun control states like California, New Jersey and Massachusetts," said Alan Gottlieb, founder of the Second Amendment Foundation. "People can't afford to spend tens of thousands of dollars on legal fees to get back a $500 firearm."

Zimmerman's article continued, reporting that perhaps one of the greatest gun confiscations occurred in New Orleans, just after Hurricane Katrina in 2005. The then mayor, Ray Nagin, ordered police to confiscate all weapons registered by New Orleans citizens. Of course, many other weapons were not registered. In fear of reprisal by the police, those residents abandoned their non-registered weapon when they fled from the water devastation. Nagin's order was eventually overturned but many citizens lost most of their duly-authorized weapons and were never compensated.

Zimmerman's article presented many other examples of gun control and gun confiscation disguised in other methods:

"Some guns confiscated for various reasons in Massachusetts are stored in a private storage company. In many instances, when the owners are allowed to retrieve their weapons, the storage fee is too high to reclaim them.

Minnesota, Wisconsin, Louisiana and Kentucky have laws that allow weapons to be confiscated from those merely accused of domestic violence - before any conviction. This means guns can be confiscated merely by accusation.

Another case was reported in Ohio where a U.S. Army veteran had weapons valued at over $10,000 confiscated from her home while she wasn't there, supposedly based on her treatment at a VA hospital. Although no charges were ever filed against her, she had to endure an expensive lawsuit to have her weapons returned.

"These tactics are a way for police departments or the government to make it more costly to own guns," said John Lott, an economist, leading expert on guns, and author at the Crime Prevention Research Center. Lott believes the illegal policies most hurt poor gun owners, who not only are less likely to afford to get their property back, but also typically live in neighborhoods where they are more vulnerable to crime.

"Seizing legally owned guns can also be a way for law enforcement agencies to boost their revenue if, as in some cases, they sell the firearms rather than destroying them," Lott said. End of Zimmerman's article.

There is sufficient evidence, adequate examples, and almost certain proof that our government, especially our federal government, does not want private citizens to own private weapons. We must ask why; why does our federal government, particularly a government controlled by Democrats, and many other bureaucracies and powerful individuals not want us (America) to be armed to protect ourselves?

Every competent American citizen must own a weapon of defense; and for three important reasons:

1. A citizen must not be unprotected against home invaders and others who intend to do them harm. The home invader or invaders would come armed to create danger. Should the victim not have at least an equal opportunity to defend himself or herself?

Gun control proponents propose this answer should be 'no,' that a home-invasion victim should merely stand and allow himself or herself to be killed by gunshot, knife wound, strangulation or other trauma. Do gun control proponents suggest the evil people should be allowed to perpetuate their evil against others without potential peril to themselves? What is their answer to protecting oneself against this personal danger? Their usual answer is to 'call the police.' How can one call the police if he or she has bullet holes through them as they bleed to death? Gun control zealots have never given a reasonable answer to this question - **and they never will**.

2. All competent American citizens must be armed to demonstrate resolve against anyone or any nation who would attack us. At this time the clear and present danger of attack is by Islamic terrorists who would make their evil provocations to create fear and test our national resolve. This is a dangerous time with a high threat of fear attacks. Their random attacks would be to create fear and disrupt our normal way of life, not necessarily to conquer us militarily. That could be a future consideration, but not at this time. A serious and deep military

threat to our homeland would more likely involve conspiracy and treason and would be facilitated by a higher order.

The concept, the very idea of America, is a threat to many leaders and many nations that rule by fear, intimidation, and theocratic ideology, such as those led by Islamic dogma. Within these realms any thoughts or ideas of deviation from dictates of the leaders or imposed religion would create a crisis from within. Within their designs, free countries such as the United States must be shown as weak and vulnerable.

They must attack with isolated terrorists, and they will, just to demonstrate they are strong enough to do it. Simply, it's to demonstrate their imitation superiority, and to create fear that will make us more vulnerable; with counter actions against ourselves. This is the first of the 'two-headed' Islamic attacks. It will be considered in the next article.

3. And, we must not forget the original purpose for the Second Amendment; to defend our great nation against a tyrannical government that would attempt to ignore our Constitution, and gain control of our nation by force - by arms if necessary. Now, one might suggest that could never happen in a free and democratic nation like ours; we are unique throughout history; we all understand and love freedom, even those who are elected to rule over us. Many have a deep feeling that our freedom and our right to pursue prosperity and happiness are God-given rights that would never be taken away; certainly not in our great nation.

Our Founding Fathers recognized this potential and ominous danger. They recognized it; they stared it right in the eyes; they understood evil will always exist and waits for an opportunity to have its own way. Why shouldn't we recognize these things? History has been long and deep; our existence has been only a brief blink in that long history. We are as vulnerable as the Romans after their thousand year reign. Evil and danger lurk around every corner of change. Our great nation is always in the flow of change. Now, let's consider the first head of that evil snake; terror threats.

Chapter 2
Terrorist Attacks

Many citizens, especially those who claim citizens should not have the right to own weapons to protect themselves, scoff at the suggestion that terrorists could ever cause a serious threat to the Untied States. Are they serious? Do they have their heads stuck in the sand? No; they have their heads buried deep in the darkest mud - or somewhere even closer in their own anatomy.

Obviously, those who fight so hard to keep citizens from having their weapons for defense have never owned a weapon; and have never had the opportunity to earn the respect weapons require. They simply don't comprehend that weapons require respect and understanding. Weapons don't think and act for themselves - by themselves. They are tools. All tools must have respect, and those who use them are expected to use them responsibly. A firearm is simply a tool to discourage, and if need be, to destroy one head of a two-headed enemy who plans to destroy us.

Let's use an example that perhaps even the most hardened gun-control advocate might understand. Let's consider a hammer.

When one thinks of a hammer one ordinarily thinks of a nail. As a person unskilled in using a firearm, one unskilled in using a hammer might suffer discomfort or harm trying to use a hammer on a nail. Perhaps one unskilled in using a hammer or unknowledgeable of hammers might think a hammer is used for just a nail. But, there are different sizes and weights of hammers as there are different sizes and strengths of nails. For simplicity, let's let Bob Vila from Bobvila.com explain hammers:

"Today, there are hammers of a dozen or more different designs manufactured for many kinds of tasks, which will be discussed below.

In general, hammers of the same kind are identified by their differing sizes, as a twenty-four-ounce hammer, for example, is larger (and heavier) than a sixteen-ounce hammer. The weight referred to is that of the hammer's head rather than the tool's overall weight.

No matter the size, every household needs at least one hammer. Whether it's for tacking a picture onto the wall or re-nailing a floorboard or piece of molding, the hammer should come quickly and easily to hand.

Claw Hammers: For most of us, this is the design we reach for when we need a hammer. Its head has a face that is used to drive nails; the peen opposite the face is a two-pronged claw that is used to pull nails out of wood. The claw hammer is one of the carpenter's basic tools.

The head on a claw hammer is made of steel, the handle of fiberglass, wood (commonly hickory, a tough, springy wood), or steel. Fiberglass and steel hammers typically have rubber, plastic, or vinyl handles for comfort and shock absorption.

Claw hammers can be purchased in many sizes, ranging from small tack hammers weighing only a few ounces to large framing hammers (designed for driving large nails) that have heads weighing up to twenty-eight ounces and handles reaching eighteen inches in length. The shape of the claw varies from one hammer to another. Larger hammers often have a flattened claw, and sometimes are referred to as wrecking or rip hammers because the claw can be used to pry apart wooden elements in demolition work. Smaller hammers usually have claws with sharper curves.

A moderate-sized hammer with a head of sixteen ounces and handle of sixteen inches will perform a wide variety of tasks, though for framing work a heavier hammer, perhaps of twenty ounces, will offer added power. (I'd suggest you leave the really big ones to those who frame buildings for a living; in the hands of the occasional user, they are unwieldy and a liability for most jobs around the house.)

When selecting a hammer, consider the face, too. A patterned face (also called a mill face) will help prevent glancing blows, because the serrations grip the head of the nail. This is especially handy when doing work that involves forceful hammering, like framing and toe-nailing. A smooth, slightly convex (belled) face is preferable for finish work. In claw hammers, flat faces are usually an indication of second-rate goods.

Ball Peen Hammer: The claw hammer is designed for working with wood, the ball peen hammer for metalwork. Sometimes called an engineer's hammer, this tool is used to drive punches and cold chisels, set rivets, and shape metal. Its head is hardened and is less likely than a claw hammer's to chip when used to pound cold chisels. Rather than having a claw, the ball peen hammer has a flat striking surface on one face and a rounded one on the other.

Always wear safety goggles when putting the club hammer to use: Stone, masonry, or other bits of debris can easily become airborne and present a grave danger to your eyes."

Now, you might ask why I used so much space discussing hammers. The answer is simple, but perhaps surprising to many people. The hammer is viewed only as a tool by most people, but there is more to a hammer than just a 'hammer.' There are many types of hammers; and for many different purposes. Each hammer must fit for a specific purpose. As a hammer is designed for a specific purpose, so is a weapon, a firearm, designed for a purpose.

Anti-gun advocates totally ignore this principle. They claim guns should be banned because they are too dangerous for people to own. If they are that concerned about safety why don't they consider trying to ban hammers? Hammers cause more death and injury in America than do guns. This article from thenewamerican.com, written by Raven Clabough, and published 4 January, 2013 explains. The article is titled: 'FBI: More Club and Hammer Homicides Than Rifle.'

"The tragic shooting at Sandy Hook Elementary School in Newtown, Connecticut on December 14 has proven to be a reference point for opponents of the Second Amendment to propose anti-gun legislation once again. However, reports from the Federal Bureau of Investigation indicate that the focus on semi-automatic rifles is misguided. In fact, according to the

FBI, more hammers, clubs, and other blunt objects are involved in murders than rifles or shotguns.

In 2011, 323 murders were committed with a rifle and 356 with a shotgun, while a staggering 496 were committed with hammers and clubs.

Furthermore, from 2005 to 2011, more people in the United States were killed with blunt objects such as hammers and clubs, or with hands and fists, than with rifles. In many of those years, twice as many people were killed with hands and fists than with rifles. So far, the anti-gun zealots haven't made a serious attempt to ban hands and fists; but there's still time once they learn this connection.

In 2006, there were 618 murders committed with a hammer or club, while 438 murders were committed with a rifle. In 2005, 445 murders were committed with a rifle while 605 by hammers and clubs.

Also in 2011, 1,694 people were killed by "knives or cutting instruments," far more than rifles and shotguns combined.

The FBI does add, however, that the "murder by rifle" statistic could be increased slightly because non-categorized types of guns are not taken into account. However, the overall data still show that a significant number of people are being killed by hammers, clubs, and knives — and that those instances of murder continue to go up each year.

What makes these findings so interesting is that rifles have been a target of some members of Congress, most notably Senator Dianne Feinstein, who have proposed banning the AR-15, a semiautomatic rifle, the same that was reportedly used by Adam Lanza in the shooting at Sandy Hook Elementary School.

CBSDC reports, "The law currently proposed by Senator Feinstein would strengthen the expired 1994 'Assault Weapons' ban, outlaw certain rifles and handguns, and restrict 'high capacity' magazines, in addition to compulsory gun registration under the National Firearms Act."

Feinstein has never been one to disguise her disdain for the Second Amendment.

"If I could have gotten 51 votes in the Senate of the United States for an outright ban, picking up every one of them, Mr. and Mrs. America turn them all in, I would have done it. I could not do that. The votes weren't here," Feinstein told MRC-TV in a 1995 interview.

But the FBI reports have prompted some to inquire about the feverish targeting of rifles. Second Amendment analyst and investigative journalist Mike Vanderboegh, pointing to the report, wonders why rifles continue to be the constant focus of new regulation proposals when they are clearly used in a relatively small number of murders, particularly when handguns are by far the most common type of firearm used in murders, with over 6,000 handgun murders in 2011, according to the FBI.

"Why do they want to ban them? Because they are afraid of them? Why are they afraid?" Vanderboegh asked.

"I think it's because many in our government fear that those weapons might one day get turned on them when their demands become too tyrannical," Vanderboegh said. End of article.

Stated as simply as possible, so even the most hardened gun control advocates might understand, a weapon is a tool. Just as a hammer is a tool. Yes, a firearm is dangerous; but so are hammers, chainsaws, crowbars, scissors, needles and pins.

My elbow once got damaged by a chainsaw when I was a young man helping my uncle cut and haul pulpwood in Waycross, Georgia. Of course it hurt and it bled, but nobody yelled, 'Ban chainsaws.' A chainsaw, just as a hammer, is a necessary tool. Needles and pins are tools, but they can also be dangerous. One single prick may cause an infection that will kill. To my knowledge, no one has ever yelled, "Ban needles and pins."

Weapons, rifles and handguns, are tools. They are tools designed for recreation as in marksmanship, acquisition of food as in hunting, and for protection; as in home protection, personal protection, and protection of our great nation. Anyone who would try to ban personal weapons from American citizens cares nothing about the survival of our great nation. Or perhaps they are just ignorant and don't understand.

Recognizing the danger we face today from an evil two-headed snake who plans to destroy us by terrorism or by deception - both aiming toward the same goal - perhaps we must identify gun-haters with the modern politically correct approach. Perhaps we should label them ignorant rather than dangerous to our great nation.

Do we need those tools, our weapons, to protect ourselves and our nation against one head of that evil snake determined to destroy us? Current revelations suggest it's an absolute necessity that we be armed.

Reportedly, hundreds of aliens from countries other than Mexico have been flowing across our southern borders. These are identified as other than Mexicans (OTM.) Their normal routine is to flow into a South American country first and learn the Spanish language before the cross into the United States. Once across, most are never tracked to determine their final destinations or their purpose for being here. Some South American countries now are not supportive of America policies, and likely would not identify or report this dangerous activity by those aliens.

Where are they coming from? Many are coming from Egypt, Iraq, Yemen, Saudi Arabia, Pakistan, Afghanistan, and Iran. Are the numbers significant? In 2006, more than 108,000 were identified. Reportedly, that number had increased by fifty percent in 2013.

In response to long-term speculation that Islamic terrorists were partnering with drug cartels in South America to flow into the United States through our southern borders, I wrote a 350 page novel titled: 'America 20XX: The New World Order.' In the book, I described how terrorists were sneaking across the border as they assisted drug lords deliver their illegal products.

As they assisted with moving drugs, they also delivered and stock-piled weapons in tunnels north of the border; in Arizona. I based that location for the novel from my frequent trips to California, as I drive along Interstate 8 just south of Casa Grande. As I drove along the highway, I would often think what a great location to sneak across the border - it's so isolated. I began my novel's story in that location.

I published 20XX the first week of January, 2011. Two weeks later, news reports revealed a book titled, 'In Memory of our

Martyrs' was found on an isolated desert trail just south of Casa Grande. That book was published in Iran and was a compilation of biographical data of many Muslims who had committed suicide bombings. It was found by DHS agents from the Casa Grande office. (More information about that book can be found with an online inquiry, 'Martyrs Book.')

During that same time period many innocents crossing the border with them were found dead - executed. In the novel, these were innocents who learned they were smuggling not only drugs for the drug lords, but also weapons for the terrorists. They were killed to silence them.

Understanding their modus operandi, an appropriate question might be; how many are crossing over as terrorist cell members waiting for the signal to make their terror known? Another appropriate question complementing that one might be; what happened to all those weapons lost across the border through our government's magnificent 'Fast and Furious' gun operation? Was that operation a random act; or was it part of a more serious and long-term operational plan?

It's also reported that many 'no-go' zones now exist in the United States. Some have even been exposed and documented as having arms, training with those arms, training in hand-to-hand combat and enforcing Sharia law in those isolated societies. Often they are so isolated their training weapons gun shots can't be heard by anyone outside the area. Why are they here? Why are they training for military combat? Why are they creating their 'own country' withing our country? What is their ultimate aim?

Their self-isolation suggests only one thing; they do not plan to accept the conditions and responsibilities of being a United

States citizen. If they don't plan to assimilate into our society what do they plan? If they are armed, should we not be at least equally armed; with out tools to protect ourselves and our nation?

Recently, it's been reported that the threat is even growing and becoming more ominous. This is a report by Judicialwatch.org titled: 'ISIS Camp a Few Miles from Texas, Mexican Authorities Confirm.' This article was dated April 14, 2015:

"ISIS is operating a camp just a few miles from El Paso, Texas, according to Judicial Watch sources that include a Mexican Army field grade officer and a Mexican Federal Police Inspector.

The exact location where the terrorist group has established its base is around eight miles from the U.S. border in an area known as "Anapra" situated just west of Ciudad Juárez in the Mexican state of Chihuahua. Another ISIS cell to the west of Ciudad Juárez, in Puerto Palomas, targets the New Mexico towns of Columbus and Deming for easy access to the United States, the same knowledgeable sources confirm.

During the course of a joint operation last week, Mexican Army and federal law enforcement officials discovered documents in Arabic and Urdu, as well as "plans" of Fort Bliss – the sprawling military installation that houses the US Army's 1st Armored Division. Muslim prayer rugs were recovered with the documents during the operation.

Law enforcement and intelligence sources report the area around Anapra is dominated by the Vicente Carrillo Fuentes Cartel ("Juárez Cartel"), La Línea (the enforcement arm of the cartel) and the Barrio Azteca (a gang originally formed in the jails of El Paso). Cartel control of the Anapra area make it an extremely dangerous and hostile operating environment for Mexican Army and Federal Police operations.

According to these same sources, "coyotes" engaged in human smuggling – and working for Juárez Cartel – help move ISIS terrorists through the desert and across the border between Santa Teresa and Sunland Park, New Mexico. To the east of El Paso and Ciudad Juárez, cartel-backed "coyotes" are also smuggling ISIS terrorists through the porous border between Acala and Fort Hancock, Texas. These specific areas were targeted for exploitation by ISIS because of their understaffed municipal and county police forces, and the relative safe-havens the areas provide for the unchecked large-scale drug smuggling that was already ongoing.

Mexican intelligence sources report that ISIS intends to exploit the railways and airport facilities in the vicinity of Santa Teresa, NM (a US port-of-entry). The sources also say that ISIS has "spotters" located in the East Potrillo Mountains of New Mexico (largely managed by the Bureau of Land Management) to assist with terrorist border crossing operations. ISIS is conducting reconnaissance of regional universities; the White Sands Missile Range; government facilities in Alamogordo, NM; Ft. Bliss; and the electrical power facilities near Anapra and Chaparral, NM." End of article.

In summary, one head of the deadly snake, aggressive Islamic terrorists, is looking us directly in our eyes and saying, "I am coming to kill you and make your life as miserable as I can until I convert each single person in your satanic country into a Muslim." That snake is also saying, "If you do not convert and do as I command, I will kill you and cut off your head; you are unworthy of living." They threaten this in the name of their god and for that religion. Could those terrorists who threaten us with bold and open aggressive action actually conquer us militarily? Probably not.

Certainly they could not subjugate the United States militarily. Time, distance and logistics would not allow them to have enough forces or materiel to present a combative front. Any show of concentrated military might could be rapidly wiped out with a few bombs or missiles; even drones controlled on a local battlefield.

If they were to launch a military attack it would be by fast hit-and-run tactics. The purpose for those attacks would be to create fear and confusion, not to conquer militarily. Their strategic plan would be fear itself. But, what might that cause other than some loss of life? Just a few intermittent but routine fear attacks would harm our economy and our way of life.

For example, what would happen to unarmed citizens if only two or three Islamic terrorists blocked a major highway on a long stretch with no exits, and began walking along that highway shooting or beheading every person in those automobiles? If citizens were not armed, that slaughter could continue until enough armed police arrived. How long would that take? Imagine the fear and horror of those defenseless people.

What would the gun-haters say then? Perhaps they would say or suggest those private citizens should not have been on the highway, anyway, at that time. Perhaps they are the same people who would claim the drivers were polluting the atmosphere with their gasoline emissions. Seriously, would they express more concern about gun-ownership than about those people's lives and the fear and horror they experienced?

Some gun-haters are such total zealots I'm not sure what they might say.

Perhaps those zealots might change their minds if those highway blockades became so numerous that it affected the flow of economic transportation; the flow of food and other goods and services. Would they complain about the lack of produce on store shelves - or would they be more concerned that someone might accidently shoot themselves if they had a personal weapon strapped to their side? Or, might they suggest that every produce transport truck must have an armed police officer in the cab to accompany the driver?

For another example, the threat of Islamic terrorist attacks in malls throughout America has been considered and discussed. What would happen if that were to occur; if terrorists began mass killing of people in malls? Would it not take only a few of those attacks to disrupt normal commerce in our society. How many people would become too fearful to go to malls to shop - even if those malls had many posted security guards. How quickly could security guards or sufficiently-armed police arrive?

These questions would create so much fear from normal shoppers that sales and commerce - and our economy - would suffer. How many jobs would be lost? How much despair would be created?

Simply, it's not the actual terrorist attacks within our nation that would devastate our nation. It's the fear that would devastate our nation the most. We could kill all the terrorists that attack us; but could we destroy the fear they would create? Could we live normally in a free America constantly surrounded by and attacked by fear? Even worse, that fear would justify proclamation of martial law within our great nation. Many citizens would support that action. It would seem the sensible thing to do at that time. Once created, would that power of martial law ever be relinquished back to the guidance of our Constitution?

Attacks by terrorists must be feared. But, it's the fear itself that's more likely to create the greater disaster; the loss of a nation.

Chapter 3
The Islamic 'Whore'

My recent book, 'The War On Christians' begins: "Is there now a war against Christians? If so, who is waging this war and who are its leaders?" Who is involved in this war and how does it affect us? I will repeat that information here in this book since it's so critical to current events.

Yes, there's a clear and definitive war against Christians and other related religions such as Jewish. In reality, this war taking place now is the same war prophesied in the Bible, in the Book of Revelation. That war is taking place before our very eyes as Islamic terrorists and other militants annihilate people and destroy lands and ancient artifacts while they raze humanity from the earth in their crazed rant in the Middle East.

This war was prophesied two thousand years ago by the Apostle John as he wrote the Book of Revelation while he was exiled on the island of Patmos. Patmos is still there in its same location just off the coast of Turkey. It's near the ancient city of Ephesus, one of the seven biblical churches, and the location where many of Jesus's disciples taught while that area was called Asia. Although cryptic, Chapter 12 in the Book of

Revelation explains the beginning of this war on Christianity and its cause. The numbers below are the verse numbers:

"And there appeared a great wonder in heaven; a woman clothed with the sun, and the moon under her feet, and upon her head a crown of twelve stars.

2. And she being with child cried, travailing in birth, and pained to be delivered.

3. And there appeared another wonder in heaven; and behold a great red dragon, having seven heads and ten horns, and seven crowns upon his heads.

4. And his tail drew the third part of the stars of heaven, and did cast them to the earth: and the dragon stood before the woman which was ready to be delivered, for to devour her child as soon as it was born.

5. And she brought forth a man child, who was to rule all nations with a rod of iron:..

6. And the woman fled into the wilderness, where she hath a place prepared of God,...

7. And there was war in heaven: Michael and his angels fought against the dragon; and the dragon fought and his angels,

8. And prevailed not; neither was their place found any more in heaven.

9. And the great dragon was cast out, that old serpent, called the Devil, and Satan, which deceiveth the whole world: he was cast out into the earth, and his angels were cast out with him.

13. And when the dragon saw that he was cast unto the earth, he persecuted the woman which brought forth the man child.

14. And to the woman were given two wings of a great eagle, that she might fly into the wilderness, into her place, where she is nourished for a time, and times, and half a time, from the face of the serpent.

17. And the dragon was wroth with the woman, and went to make war with the remnant of her seed, which keep the commandments of God, and have the testimony of Jesus Christ."

A summary: The known world at that time, primarily Rome, knew the Jews were expecting a messiah even before Jesus was born. They waited for him, and at the expected time had all newborn males killed hoping one would be that expected messiah. This mass killing is known as the 'Massacre of the Innocents,' by Herod the Great, the Roman appointed King of the Jews. It included the execution of all young male children in the vicinity of Jerusalem. "upon her head a crown of twelve stars" likely refers to the twelve Jewish tribes at that time.

Verse 14 seems most cryptic until 'two wings of a great eagle' is understood. Jews and Christians were totally persecuted until a 'great eagle' suddenly adopted Christianity as the world religion. Constantine the 'Great' who ruled from 306-337 adopted Christianity after a vision he had in 312 that he attributed to helping him win a great battle against a major enemy. It was the Battle of Milvian Bridge.

According to writings, before the battle Constantine looked into the sun and saw a cross of light, with the words, "in this sign, conquer." He had his men paint a cross on their shields before the battle; that resulted in a major victory. As a result, he adopted Christianity for the Roman Empire. Soon afterward, his mother, Saint Helena, made many pilgrimage trips to the Holy Land identifying and preserving special Christian landmarks. This was the beginning of the Roman Catholic Church.

What about the 'two wings of a great eagle?' These are the words that allow important parts of Revelation to be interpreted. Without this understanding nothing else makes any sense. An eagle with two widespread wings was the standard symbol for the Roman Empire. It was proudly carried on a tall staff ahead of marching troops; including King Constantine.

Verse 14 presents critical information that explains events happening today, especially regarding the bloody tirade by radical Islamists throughout the world. It contains the words, "... where she is nourished for a time, and times, and half a time, from the face of the serpent."

This information is basically the key that unlocks two great mysteries. Considering this biblical information inside real-world history clarifies events that could not have been seen or interpreted much earlier than our present time. That time sequence could not have been interpreted before certain events happened. Now, they have happened and they can be interpreted..

By connecting and interpreting the information in Chapter 12, it's clear that the 'woman' described is a religion. And, that religion is Christianity. Once 'two wings of a great eagle' is interpreted, it becomes clear that Rome, Constantine at that time, protected that religion. The Roman Empire continued to protect that religion. But, what happened after the 'time, and times, and half a time?' The answer is unlocked with the keys of 'time.'

Constantine's battle at Milvian Bridge occurred in 312 A.D. It's reasonable to believe, after purges and indoctrination, Christianity became fully adopted within the Roman Empire approximately 350 A.D. which is the key to interpreting the times information; 'time, and times, and half a time.' In this case a time would be a hundred years. Addition of this information would indicate that total time must be 350 years. No other time suggestions are given. Since recorded history of that time is not precise (for example the exact date Christians came under the protection of Rome) approximations must be used for calculating.

When did Islam become established? You guessed it; approximately 350 years later. Although Muhammed had his first vision that began Islam in 310 A.D. the religion didn't become fully established until much later, perhaps between 600 and 700 A.D. A formal date has never been established. It became a warrior class that began persecuting and killing Christians at that time.

Two points are critical here to identify Islam as the serpent that would attack Christians 350 years after Christianity was protected by Rome. The first point is the recognition of the 350 year identity time. Second is the introduction of the other woman, religion, also revealed in the Book of Revelation. In summary, Rome gave protection to Christianity approximately 350 A.D.; Christians were attacked by another religion approximately 350 years later. But, who or what is that other religion? The Bible makes that answer absolutely and perfectly clear. It's identified in Revelation, Chapters 6 and 17. The description is a little lengthy, but I will include it here so it's not necessary to dig your Bible out of your closet. Let's begin with Chapter 17.

In the first verse an angel carries John, in the spirit, to show him the judgement of the 'great whore that sitteth upon many waters.' This was at the conclusion of several prophetic disasters. Verse 3 adds, "So he carried me away into the wilderness; and I saw a woman sit upon a scarlet coloured beast, full of names of blasphemy, having seven heads and ten horns." Verse 4 continues; "And the woman was arrayed in purple and scarlet color, and decked with gold and precious stones and pearls, having a golden cup in her hand full of abominations and filthiness of her fornication:" 5; And upon her forehead was a name written, Mystery, Babylon the great mother of harlots and abominations of the earth." This information describes this woman as a respected religion, "arrayed in purple and scarlet colour." Purple is the color of royalty and respect. The scarlet color will be explained shortly.

Once it's understood that this woman, as was the first woman, is a religion, Verse 6 describes this religion. "And I saw the woman drunken with the blood of the saints, and with the blood of the martyrs of Jesus; and when I saw her I wondered with great admiration." Is there any doubt in anyone's mind that this description could only be that of Islam? No other religion or group is "drunken with the blood of the martyrs of Jesus." That woman is the religion that's killing and beheading Jews, Christians, and anyone else in their path of destruction that refuses to accept their beliefs. This religion is clearly: Islam.

Now, for those who doubt the words of the Bible, and its prophesy, although the above information is clearly prophesy revealed in our face, here's another item of Biblical interest. It pertains to what's happening today, even as we read and watch the news. Chapter 17 adds more. It explains another event to come; what happens to the 'mother of harlots - the whore' - those savage Islamic butchers.

When John wondered with 'great admiration' at the described woman, the angel asked why he marveled, then said he would explain more. Verse 7, "I will tell thee the mystery of the woman, and of the beast that carrieth her, which hath the seven heads and ten horns." Verse 9 adds, "The seven heads are seven mountains, on which the woman sitteth." (I now interpret these seven mountains as the seven continents upon which Islam has spread.)

Verse 12, "And the ten horns which thou sawest are ten kings, which have received no kingdom as yet; but receive power as kings one hour with the beast." That beast that will give them 'power' is not revealed; perhaps a provider of air strikes, manpower and logistics?

Verse 16 suggests the prophetic part. "And the ten horns which thou sawest upon the beast, these shall hate the whore, and shall make her desolate and naked, and shall eat her flesh, and burn her with fire." Does this not suggest that ten Islamic kings (they have already been identified) will battle and defeat the 'whore?'

The whore has already been identified as ruthless killers. Are there not ten Islamic countries now fighting against ISIS (radical Muslims) and other terrorists in the Middle East? If not prophetic, one must admit it's very interesting how closely the Bible describes what's happening today. And, Revelation was written by John 2000 years ago.

43

Now, remember this quote above, "and I saw a woman sit upon a scarlet coloured beast, full of names of blasphemy, having seven heads and ten horns?" That woman was described again in Chapter 6, Verse 4; only this time the scarlet coloured beast was described as a red horse: "And there went out another horse that was red; and power was given to him that sat thereon to take peace from the earth, and that they should kill one another; and there was given unto him a great sword."

Does Islam have any prophesies revealed such as those from the Christian Bible? Absolutely not. It's only prophetic that the demonic actions by Islam is fully revealed in the Bible centuries before Islam was founded. The list below is an example of their determined and evil-based terrorism. The information is taken from Wikipedia:

September 11, 2012 – 2012 Benghazi attack on the U.S. Consulate. 4 dead, 11 injured.

February 21, 2013 – 2013 Hyderabad blasts, two bomb blasts killed 16 people and injured 119.

April 15, 2013 – Boston Marathon bombings. The blast killed 3 and injured 183 others.

May 11, 2013 – Reyhanl bombings, killed 52 people and wounded 140.

September 21, 2013 – Westgate shopping mall attack, 67 killed, 175 wounded.

September 22, 2013 – Peshawar church attack, 80–83 killed, 250 wounded.

September 29, 2013 – Gujba college massacre. 44 students killed by Boko Haram.

October 28, 2013 – A 4x4 vehicle crashed into a crowd and burst into flames in Tiananmen Square in Beijing, 5 killed, 38 wounded.

February 14, 2014 – Borno Massacre at least 200 killed by Boko Haram.

March 1, 2014 – A group of 8 individuals attacked civilians at Kunming Railway Station, 28 dead, 143 wounded.

April 30, 2014 – Two assailants attacked passengers and detonated explosives at the Ürümqi railway station, 3 dead, 79 wounded.

May 20, 2014 – Jos bombings at least 118 killed and over 56 injured.

May 22, 2014 – Two SUVs which carried 5 assailants. 39 dead, 90+ wounded.

May 24, 2014 – Jewish Museum of Belgium shooting, killing 4 people.

August 2014 – Islamic State fighters massacred some 700 people, mostly men, of the Shu'aytat tribe in Deir ez-Zor Governorate.

October 5, 2014 – Grozny bombing. 5 officers and the suicide bomber, were killed, while 12 others were wounded.

Israel October 22, 2014 – A Hamas terrorist ran his vehicle into a group killing 2 and wounding 8.

November 5, 2014 – A Hamas operative drove a van into a crowd killing 4 and wounding 13.

November 28, 2014 – Kano bombing. Around 120 people were killed and another 260 injured.

December 4, 2014 – 2014 Grozny clashes. 26 total dead, including 14 policemen.

December 16, 2014 – Peshawar school attack. Over 140 people dead, including at least 132 children.

December 16, 2014 – Two suicide car bombers rammed their vehicles into a Shiite rebels' checkpoint killing 26, including 16 students.

December 18, 2014 – Boko Haram insurgents killed 32 men and kidnapped at least 185 women and children.

December 18, 2014 – Mass grave of 230 Tribesmen killed by Islamic State found in Eastern Syria.

December 22, 2014 – Boko Haram insurgents bombed a bus station in the city of Gombe, killing at least twenty people.

December 2014 – Islamic State militants execute 150 women of Al-Anbar, some of whom were pregnant at the time.

December 24, 2014 – A suicide bomber killed 33 people and wounded 55 others in Madaen, south of Baghdad.

Somalia December 25, 2014 – Al-Shabaab attack in Mogadishu leaves 9 dead.

December 28, 2014 – Boko Haram attacks village in Cameroon leaving 30 dead.

January 7–9, 2015 – 5 attacks in and around Paris kill 17 people, and leave 22 other people injured.

January 8, 2015 – Boko Haram attacks town of Baga in northern Nigeria killing at least 200 people. Another 2000 are unaccounted for.

January 30, 2015 – Suicide bomber kills at least 55, injuring at least 59 in a Shiite mosque in southern Pakistan.

February 13, 2015 – Heavily armed militants killed at least 19 people and wounded more than 40 after they stormed into a Shiite mosque.

March 15, 2015 – Suicide bombers kill at least 15 people in attacks on two churches in Lahore.

March 18, 2015 – Militants linked to Islamic State attack the Bardo National Museum with guns, killing 21 people and injuring around 50.

March 20, 2015 – 135 killed in bombings on several mosques by Islamic State.

April 2, 2015 – 148 killed in Al-Shabaab's Garissa University.

April 17, 2015 – A series of bombings by the Islamic State occurred through Baghdad. 40+ killed 59+ injured.

April 17, 2015 – A car bomb exploded at the entrance of the US consulate in Erbil, Iraq. Islamic State took credit for the attack. 3 killed 5 wounded.

April 18, 2015 – A suicide bomb detonated in front of a bank in Jalalabad, Afghanistan. Islamic State claims responsibility. 33 killed 100+ injured. End of list from Wikipedia.

This is an article from almanar.com (AFP Source), November, 2014 that shows another look at the radical Islamic horror. This is another look at the actions by the 'whore' who rides the scarlet beast and the red horse, described in Revelation. It's titled: 'ISIL Terrorists Killing Christians, Beheading Children in Iraq.'

"The Islamic State of Iraq and the Levant (ISIL) terrorist group has continued its effort to destroy the Christian faith in Iraq, as reports come out revealing the extensive killing of Christians, including crucifixions and the beheadings of children. They are systemically beheading children, and mothers, and fathers. The world hasn't seen an evil like this for a generation. 'There's actually a park in Mosul that they've actually beheaded children and put their heads on a stick,' Mark Arabo, national spokesman for Iraqi Christians told CNN.

According to a report by Arab News, ISIL militants have moved on from beheading to burying women and children alive in mass graves.

In July, the ISIL captured Mosul, Iraq's second largest city, as they looted Christian homes, desecrated cemeteries, destroyed tombs of biblical prophets, ruined churches, and pulled down crosses.

Christians were told that they could escape this harassment and death by paying a fine. However, Arabo says the ISIL broke this so-called promise.

"The letter that they sent out with those three items (convert, pay a fine or die), they did ask to pay a fine but actually after they pay a fine, they (ISIL militants) are actually taking over their wives and their daughters and making them into their wives. So really it's convert or die, face death by the sword," explained Arabo.

"They've marked the red stamp of death on Christian homes and basically saying we know who you are and if you come back, you will get killed. That's why we're saying this is a Christian holocaust within our midst and the world community cannot turn a blind eye," said Arabo. "They are absolutely killing every Christian they see. This is a genocide in every sense of the word. They want everyone to convert and they want Sharia law to be the law of the land." End of article.

This is another article from eaglerising.com, written by Onan Coca, July 2014. It's titled, Muslim Terrorists Declare "Sexual Jihad" Raping and Killing Christians. It details further atrocities against Christians. It begins:

"Muslim 'holy' warriors are taking the war to innocent women and children, having declared a sexual jihad on women of the Middle East. ISIS terrorists in Iraq and Syria have begun pulling women and girls from their homes and raping them whenever they feel the need.

The Iraq High Commission for Human Rights is reporting that ISIS has begun demanding a poll tax (or jizya) from Christians in Iraq. Christians who cannot pay the tax are in terrible danger;

one family who could not pay was attacked by ISIS terrorists who raped the mother and daughter in front of the husband/father. He was so distraught that he committed suicide.

Another report from the area said that ISIS had murdered four Christian women for not wearing traditional Islamic veils.

ISIS is spewing its evil filth all over the Iraqi and Syrian countryside and no one is safe from them – whether Muslim or Christian. But the evil ISIS monsters seem to take particular joy in hurting innocent women and children. The Christian enclave of Bartella, just outside of Mosul, is bathed in fear as they await the oncoming ISIS onslaught.

Just outside the militants' control, and desperately vulnerable to attack an attack by ISIS, sits Bartella. Williams says Christians have inhabited the town for almost 2,000 years. The locals still pray in Aramaic, the language spoken by Jesus.

The Iraqi government soldiers who were supposed to be protecting this area ran away from the Islamic extremists. Now, Bartella is defended by about 600 lightly armed Christian militiamen. Captain Firaz Jacob is in charge, and he told CBS News everyone in the town is frightened.

When asked what they will do if the militants attack Bartella, Jacob responded with trepidation. "I don't know, but maybe they'll do what they've done in other places and kill us."

Reports of the grotesque actions of ISIS are pouring out from all over Iraq. The Organization of Women's Freedom in Iraq (OWFI) has reported a multitude of cases similar to the ones above. The organization has noted that those most at risk are displaced families without husbands or fathers to lead them. ISIS and other Islamic militants seem to seek them out almost magnetically as they search for people to victimize."

These are only a few of the many examples and reports of the evil and prophetic horror inflicted by the Islamic 'whore' described in Chapter 17 in the Book of Revelation. This horror, this whore, however is only one head of the two-headed Islamic beast that plans to destroy America and the world. To accomplish that, they must destroy everything good and precious blocking their way to their supreme evil.

Chapter 4
The Silent Jihad

While one head of the evil serpent violently attacks us, and threatens more attacks against us, the other head slips in the back door to institutionalize its ugly evil. The Muslim Brotherhood had wide, deep and long tentacles that reach into every nook and cranny to destroy our freedom, our democracy, and our future well-being.

According to Civilus Defendus 'with a hat tip to Kali Politus' at Wordpress.com, there's a standard process of Islamic encroachment to occupy and take over a non-Islamic nation. The article is titled, '4 Stages of Islamic Conquest.' To review the full plan by the Muslim Brotherhood to conquer non-Muslim nations by the process they call 'settlement' review the information at this link. It's from a Muslim Brotherhood plan discovered in 1991, titled, 'An Explanatory Memorandum: On the General Strategic Goal for the Group In North America.'

http://www.discoverthenetworks.org/viewSubCategory.asp?id=1235

Those four stages reported by Wordpress.com and the tactics to enforce or implement those stages are explained:

The first stage is infiltration.

In this stage Muslims begin moving into non-Muslim countries. Their numbers gradually increase at first, and with little or no visible conflicts. Those conflicts that exist are, at first, very subtle. They begin to fit in and ask the host country to be more understanding since they are peaceful, and only victims or where they came from. They continue to claim they are peaceful, although more conflicts between cultures continue to rise. They appeal for more tolerance.

As the size and numbers of more Muslim families increase, they begin to increase in their population and influence; more mosques are built to support those larger populations. Then those mosques become the birthplaces to spread more Islam and to begin exclaiming the stronger Islamic ideologies, and more hatred for the host countries and the historical culture of those host countries.

Once partially established as a part of the community they claim they are being persecuted by 'Islamophobia' and increase their insistence that anyone using Islamophobia against them should be charged with a hate crime. Their further reaction is to threaten legal action against individuals and groups for discrimination and hate crimes. Finally, they propose more interfaith discussions for a better understanding between religions. This is the subterfuge toward more Islamic indoctrination to continue their 'settlement.'

The Wordpress article continues:

"How many nations are suffering from Islamic infiltration? One? A handful? Nearly every nation? The Islamic leadership of the Muslim Brotherhood and others wish to dissolve each nation's sovereignty and replace it with the global imposition of Islamic sharia law. Sharia law, based on the koran, sira and hadith, condemns liberty and forbids equality and is inconsistent with the laws of all Western nations. As the author and historian Serge Trifkovic states:

'The refusal of the Western elite class to protect their nations from jihadist infiltration is the biggest betrayal in history.'"

The second stage is consolidation of power.

This is the phase, the stage where Muslim 'settlers' begin to make their presence more obvious; where they begin to demand more rights, more Islamic freedom, and more acceptance from the local society - although they try to separate themselves through that acceptance. This is as absurd as a Muslim female asking to be free in that Muslim society in which she exists. To stress this point further this is a good time to ask that question:

(If a Muslim female is subjected by Islamic doctrine to be assaulted, maimed, abused, disregarded as a human, and actually killed, in the name of Islam - how can Islam proclaim itself to be 'The religion of Peace?" No other religion, no other country, no other real human being in this world would consider those actions as acts of 'peace.' By its own writings and proclamations, Islamists destroy the foundational basis of their existence. How could terrorizing one person, a female, or a whole nation be considered an act of 'peace?')

That Wordpress article adds this list of accelerated activities by the new Muslim communities:

"Muslim immigrants and host country converts continue demands for accommodation in employment, education, social services, financing and courts."

Even further: Proselytizing increases; Establishment and Recruitment of Jihadi cells begin; There are increased efforts to convert alienated segments of the population to Islam; Muslim leaders revise history to create more Islam into our backgrounds, and they begin to destroy the real evidence that exposes what true Islam really is.

Other subversive and 'settlement' activities include: Increasing negative propaganda against Western history; sweeping up other anti-American groups to give more strength to their operations and tactics against American status-quo. They also begin to infiltrate school systems and other teaching and influencing areas to bring children into their Islamic ideology for continued expansion of their mission. Their settlement strategies and tactics never let up; they continue onward to fulfill that grand design of world Islamism.

They increase their charge to silence their non-Muslims detractors opponents by intimidation and by other charges, such as blasphemy against Islam. They increase their emphasis and growing influence to push for more hate laws against those who oppose their plan and expose their real purpose; which is to make the land they occupy into a purely Muslim nation. According to their own writings and ideologies, they cannot be real Muslims if they stray from this final goal. Activities in this second stage also include the following:

* Efforts to introduce blasphemy and hate laws in order to silence critics.

* Continued focus on enlarging Muslim population by increasing Muslim births and immigration.

* Use of charities to recruit supporters and fund jihad.

* Covert efforts to bring about the destruction of host society from within.

* Development of Muslim political base in non-Muslim host society.

* Islamic Financial networks fund political growth, acquisition of land.

* Highly visible assassination of critics aimed to intimidate opposition.

* Tolerance of non-Muslims diminishes.

* Greater demands to adopt strict Islamic conduct.

* Clandestine amassing of weapons and explosives in hidden locations.

* Overt disregard/rejection of non-Muslim society's legal system, culture.

* Efforts to undermine and destroy power base of non-Muslim religions including and especially Jews and Christians.

Is there a pattern here? Theo van Gogh is murdered in the Netherlands for 'insulting' Islam; the Organization of the Islamic Conference demands 'anti-blasphemy' laws through the United Nations; France is set afire regularly by 'youths' (read Muslims); the rise of (dis-) honor killings...holocaust denial...anti-Semitism...deception re the tenets of Islam; hatred toward Christians and Jews and Hindus and Buddhists. The pattern for all to see is the rise of Islamic intolerance and the covert/cultural jihad to remake host societies into sharia-compliant worlds – to remove host sovereignty and replace it with Islamic sharia law. Sharia law that condemns earthly liberty and individual freedom, that forbids equality among faiths and between the sexes, that rejects the concept of nations outside the global house of Islam, that of dar al-Islam. That Wordpress article continues with an explanation of stage three of the Islamization process.

Stage 3: Open War with Leadership and Culture

* Open violence to impose Sharia law and associated cultural restrictions; rejection of host government, subjugation of other religions and customs.

* Intentional efforts to undermine the host government & culture.

* Acts of barbarity to intimidate citizens and foster fear and submission.

* Open and covert efforts to cause economic collapse of the society.

* All opposition is challenged and either eradicated or silenced.

* Mass execution of non-Muslims.

* Widespread ethnic cleansing by Islamic militias.

* Rejection and defiance of host society secular laws or culture.

* Murder of "moderate" Muslim intellectuals who don't support Islamization.

* Destruction of churches, synagogues and other non-Muslim institutions.

* Women are restricted further in accordance with Sharia law.

* Large-scale destruction of population, with assassinations and bombings.

* Toppling of government and usurpation of political power.

* Imposition of Sharia law.

The website www.thereligionofpeace.com keeps track of the number of violent jihad attacks as best it can. The site lists more than 14,000 attacks since September 2001. It is worth a visit. What is occurring, however, that is likely inestimable are events where muslims are bullied by other muslims for not being "muslim enough," where non-Muslims are intimidated into doing or not doing what they desire, where remnant populations are in a death spiral simply for being non-muslim in a predominantly muslim area. Christians, Jews, Hindus, Buddhists Animists and Atheists meet with death, property destruction or confiscation, forced conversion, rape, excessive taxation (the jizya), enslavement, riotous mobs and various other forms of islam (in-) justice at the hands of muslims in

Sudan, Philippines, Kenya, Malaysia, India, etc. And let us not forget 'death to Apostates' the world over.

Stage 4: Totalitarian Islamic "Theocracy."

Islam becomes the only religious-political-judicial-cultural ideology:

* Sharia becomes the "law of the land.

* All non-Islamic human rights are cancelled.

* Enslavement and genocide of non-Muslim population.

* Freedom of speech and the press eradicated.

* All religions other than Islam are forbidden and destroyed.

* Destruction of all evidence of non-Muslim culture, populations and symbols in country (Buddhas, houses of worship, art, etc).

The House of Islam ("peace"), dar al-Islam, includes those nations that have submitted to Islamic rule, to the soul crushing, liberty-condemning, discriminatory law of Sharia. The rest of the world is in the House of War, dar al-harb, because it does not submit to Sharia, and exists in a state of rebellion or war with the will of 'Allah.' No non-Muslim state or its citizens are "innocent," and remain viable targets of war for not believing in 'Allah.'

The Christian, Jewish, Coptic, Hindu and Zoroastrian peoples of the world have suffered under subjugation for centuries. The Dhimmi-esque are forbidden to construct houses of worship or repair existing ones, economically crippled by the heavy jizya (tax), socially humiliated, legally discriminated against, criminally targeted and generally kept in a permanent state of weakness, fear and vulnerability by Islamic governments.

It should be noted that forced conversions (Egypt) and slavery (Sudan) are still reported. Homosexuals have been hung in the public square in Iran. Young girls are married to old men. Apostates are threatened with death. "Honor" killings are routine. Women are legally second-class citizens, though Muslim males insist they are "treated better" than in the West. These more obvious manifestations may distract from some less obvious ones such as the lack of intellectual inquiry in science, narrow scope of writing, all but non-existent art and music, sexual use and abuse of youth and women, and the disregard for personal fulfillment, joy and wonder. Look into the eyes of a recently married 12 year old girl to see the consequence of the moral deprivation spawned by Islam.

End of article by Wordpress.com.

This information above explains the stages and steps as Muslims encroach and replace the foundations and cultures of a sovereign nation. But, how do they achieve these steps; how do they position themselves to accomplish those tactics? Their process is not secret. Muslim leadership have already boldly proclaimed how they will do it. Their plan is clearly laid out in the document introduced above, the Explanatory Memorandum. That memorandum describes the process of 'Settlement.' It's also commonly known as the 'silent Jihad' or the 'third Jihad.'

Although it's a silent Jihad, it's more dangerous and effective against our democracy and freedom than is their terrorist approach. The terror head of the two-headed snake is the distraction; while the silent part of the two-headed snake silently wraps its body in a death grip around our freedom. That deadly snake is already closer than one can imagine.

Muslims have that long-range plan to transpose America into a total Islamic country "without firing a single shot." This plan is already active and is far along in its program.

This Muslim Brotherhood plan was discovered in 1991, titled, 'An Explanatory Memorandum: On the General Strategic Goal for the Group In North America.' Just take a casual look around and you will see how far they have already progressed in this effort. Many Islamists connected to the Muslim Brotherhood are already in powerful positions in our government - including important advisory positions to the 'President of the United States.' This is how that document (Memorandum) begins:

"An Explanatory Memorandum"
On the General Strategic Goal for the Group In North
America 5/22/1991

Contents:

An introduction in explanation
The Concept of Settlement
The Process of Settlement
Comprehensive Settlement Organizations

Subject: A project for an explanatory memorandum for the General Strategic goal for the Group in North America mentioned in the long-term plan.

One: The Memorandum is derived from:

The general strategic goal of the Group in America which was approved by the Shura Council and the Organizational Conference for the year [1987] is "Enablement of Islam in North America, meaning: establishing an effective and a stable Islamic Movement led by the Muslim Brotherhood which adopts Muslims' causes domestically and globally, and which works to expand the observant Muslim base, aims at unifying and directing Muslims' efforts, presents Islam as a civilization alternative, and supports the global Islamic State wherever it is". The priority that is approved by the Shura Council for the work of the Group in its current and former session which is "Settlement". The positive development with the brothers in the Islamic Circle in an attempt to reach a unity of merger. The constant need for thinking and future planning, an attempt to read it and working to "shape" the present to comply and suit the needs and challenges of the future."

This is only a sampling of a long document. The full 18-page text may be read online by searching: 'An Explanatory Memorandum.' According to the document, the plan would include these organizations and all others in the United States associated with Islam as part of the 'settlement' plan:

ISNA	ISLAMIC SOCIETY OF NORTH AMERICA
MSA	MUSLIM STUDENTS' ASSOCIATION
MCA	THE MUSLIM COMMUNITIES ASSOCIATION
AMSS	THE ASSOCIATION OF MUSLIM SOCIAL SCIENTISTS
AMSE	THE ASSOCIATION OF MUSLIM SCIENTISTS AND ENGINEERS
IMA	ISLAMIC MEDICAL ASSOCIATION
ITC	ISLAMIC TEACHINC CENTER
NAIT	NORTH AMERICAN ISLAMIC TRUST
FID	FOUNDATION FOR INTERNATIONAL DEVELOMENT
IHC	ISLAMIC HOUSING COOPERATIVE
ICD	ISLAMIC CENTERS DIVISION

ATP   AMERICAN TRUST PUBLICATIONS
AVC   AUDIO-VISUAL CENTER
IBS   ISLAMIC BOOK SERVICE
MBA   MUSLIM BUSINESSMEN ASSOCIATION
MYNA   MUSLIM YOUTH OF NORTH AMERICA
IFC   ISNA FIQH COMMITTEE
IPAC   ISNA POLITICAL AWARENESS COMMITTEE
IED   ISLAMIC EDUCATION DEPARTMENT
MAYA   MUSLIM ARAB YOUTH ASSOCIATION
MISG   MALASIAN ISLAMIC STUDY GROUP
IAP   ISLAMIC ASSOCIATION FOR PALESTINE
UASR   UNITED ASSOCIATION FOR STUDIES AND RESEARCH
OLF   OCCUPIED LAND FUND
MIA   MERCEY INTERNATIONAL ASSOCIATION
ICNA   ISLAMIC CIRCLE OF NORTH AMERICA
BMI   BA1TUL MAL INC
IIIT   INTERNATIONAL INSTITUTE FOR ISLAMIC THOUCHT
IIC   ISLAMIC INFORMATION CENTER

This is another link to that 18-page 'Settlement' document:

http://www.clarionproject.org/Muslim_Brotherhood_Explan atory_Memorandum

To summarize that document, it gives long and detailed instructions regarding every part of our American society. It covers infiltration into the arts and sciences, education, social clubs, social networking, and any other place one can imagine squeezing into to create a footprint that can later be used to bring the whole Muslim Brotherhood project together. In short, it suggests to 'be nice' and participate, then when the stage is set to begin taking more control over that particular area.

Our current administration under Barack Obama seems not only to be cooperating with that plan, but also appears in many ways to be part of the plan itself. The Muslim Brotherhood has already worked itself into a strong foothold in the federal administration as well as into our education systems. Obama paves the way for them to advance.

Chapter 5
Islamic Infiltration

Barack Hussein Obama supports every Muslim activity taking place to integrate Muslim activities within every nook and cranny in America. This is directly in accordance with that Explanatory Memorandum. Just consider how deeply he has already infiltrated high-level Muslims into our government. Only six of Obama's most important Muslim appointments are shown next, but they are typical of his many Muslim appointments to fill those important positions as reported by The 'Investigative Project on Terrorism:'

"Arif Alikhan – Assistant Secretary for Policy Development for the U.S. Department of Homeland Security. Arif Alikhan played a key role in the removal of the LAPD "Mapping" Plan which involved mapping Muslim communities in an effort to identify potential hotbeds of extremism. LAPD officials said that it was crucial for them to gain a better understanding of isolated parts of the Muslim community because those groups can potentially breed violent extremism.

Alikhan reportedly helped raise funds for Muslim Public Affairs Council (MPAC) that has labeled a deadly anti-U.S. terrorist attack a legitimate operation, referred to terrorists as "freedom fighters" and equated Muslim jihad with the sentiments of American statesman Patrick Henry. He joined MPAC on April 11 for a special fundraiser called "Be the Change" to support what the group calls its innovative leadership development programs.

Mohammed Elibiary – Homeland Security Adviser. According to information reported in an article by the Investigative Project on Terrorism, Mohamed Elibiary has defended Muslim Brotherhood luminary Sayyid Qutb, Ayatollah Khomeini, and radical New York Imam Siraj Wahhaj. He has asserted conspiracy theories, supported terror-related individuals and organizations and accused the government of mounting a war against Islam. Despite all this, he was appointed by Department of Homeland Security (DHS) Secretary Janet Napolitano to the Homeland Security Advisory Council (HSAC).

Elibiary is the co-founder, president and CEO of the Freedom and Justice Foundation (F&J), founded in November 2002 "to promote a Centrist Public Policy environment in Texas by coordinating the state level government and interfaith community relations for the organized Texas Muslim community." F&J's nonprofit status was revoked by the IRS in May 2010 for failure to file the requisite 990 forms that would reveal the entity's source of income. Similarly, according to the Texas Comptroller of Public Accounts, F&J has not filed a Texas Franchise Tax Public Information Report.

The North Texas Islamic Council (NTIC), also called the "Texas Islamic Council," is an affiliate organization of F&J. Elibiary is the registered agent for the NTIC, and one of the directors is H. Mustafaa Carroll, who is also the executive director of the Houston chapter of the Council on American-Islamic Relations (CAIR). CAIR is a Muslim Brotherhood-linked group in the U.S. that was formed as part of a Hamas-support network in the U.S.

Elibiary was a Fellow in 2008-2009 with the American Muslim Civic Leadership Institute (AMCLI), "housed at the University of Southern California's Center for Religion and Civic Culture (CRCC), which works in partnership with the Prince Alwaleed Bin Talal Center for Muslim Christian Understanding (ACMCU) at Georgetown University." This is the center where Obama had the Christian icon covered with black plywood before he made his speech there in April, 2009.

Elibiary was featured in a CNN piece in December 2009 as a "deradicalizer." He likened the allure of radicalism among American Muslim teens to "at-risk gangbangers, who want to stand up for their community, to address grievances of the global Muslim community more effectively than they've seen the elder generation."

Elibiary has defended Sayyid Qutb, the Islamist ideologue credited with inspiring the Muslim Brotherhood and terrorist groups including al-Qaida. He recommends Qutb's writing as offering "the potential for a strong spiritual rebirth that's truly ecumenical allowing all faiths practiced in America to enrich us and motivate us to serve God better by serving our fellow man more."

Rashad Hussain – Special Envoy to the (OIC) Organization of the Islamic Conference. A Global Muslim Brotherhood Daily Report took a look at Hussain's official biography and found several concerning affiliations. The first is that in October

2000, Hussain spoke at a conference sponsored by the Association of Muslim Social Scientists, which was listed in an internal Muslim Brotherhood document as one of "our organizations and the organizations of our friends," and the Prince Alwaleed Center for Muslim-Christian Understanding of Georgetown University, which receives Saudi funding and is directed by prominent Muslim Brotherhood advocate, John Esposito.

In September 2004, Hussain played a role in the Muslim Students Association's annual conference, which was founded by Muslim Brotherhood in 1963 and is also listed as one the group's fronts in its own documents. Since then, many of its nearly 600 college chapters have engaged in extremism and the group closely collaborates with the other Brotherhood fronts. For example, MSA was part of an umbrella organization called the American Muslim Taskforce that led a campaign against the FBI's use of informants in mosques and accused the agency of anti-Muslim activity. Several Brotherhood affiliates are in this including the Muslim-American Society, the Islamic Circle of North America, the Islamic Society of North America, the Muslim Public Affairs Council and the Council on American-Islamic Relations.

At this conference, Hussain spoke alongside the daughter of Professor Sami Al-Arian, who was convicted of being a key leader of the Palestinian Islamic Jihad terrorist group and later admitted to being a member of the Muslim Brotherhood. Hussain also defended Al-Arian and described his prosecution as being a "politically-motivated persecution."

The network of Brotherhood-affiliated groups has consistently been on his side throughout the entire ordeal and celebrated his release. Interestingly, the story in The Washington Report on

Middle East Affairs that quoted Hussain's defense of Al-Arian has been altered since its original publication. A cnsnews article reports that the quote was removed "sometime after October 2007" and that the reporter who wrote the article expressed surprise but said she no longer worked at WRMEA and could not explain the edit.

Last May, Hussain spoke at a conference sponsored by several Brotherhood affiliates, including the Muslim Public Affairs Council, an organization whose extremism has been catalogued in a A series by The Investigative Project on Terrorism and the Council on American-Islamic Relations. The latter was listed by the federal government in 2007 as an 'unindicted co-conspirator' in the terrorism financing trial of The Holy Land Foundation, another Muslim Brotherhood front that was found to be financing Hamas. Its founders are former officials at the Islamic Association of Palestine, a Brotherhood front shut down for supporting Hamas and are said by the FBI to be members of the Brotherhood's Palestine Committee in the United States.

Hussain's view on the cause of terrorism is important to note as it will play a significant role in the Obama Administration's outreach to the Muslim world. He quoted a study that concluded that 'The primary cause of broad-based anger and anti-Americanism is not a clash of civilizations but the perceived effect of U.S. foreign policy in the Muslim world.' In this statement, it appears that he believes that terrorism is the product of opposition to foreign policy, rather than the product of a politico-religious totalitarian ideology, which explains his opposition to terms like "Islamic terrorism."

On the other hand, Hussein does support the use of the term "Hamas terrorists," so he cannot be said to be a supporter of

Hamas, which grew out of the Muslim Brotherhood. He has an entire section in his paper titled, 'Discrediting the Terrorist Ideology.' He opposes making democracy promotion a central part of that goal, saying that it can be interpreted as imperialism and an attempt to bring about freedom that enables immorality, but admits that it may be part of the solution. He instead suggests that the government use Muslim voices to argue that Islam forbids acts of terrorism and extremism.

One other important part of his paper is when he proposes that the U.S. build a Muslim coalition "not limited to those who advocate Western-style democracy, and avoid creating a dichotomy between freedom and Islamic society." This would set the stage for a partnership with the Muslim Brotherhood. Rather than focusing on supporting elements that will genuinely argue that democracy is compatible with Islam, his standard for allies is that they just oppose terrorism and extremism. Apparently, those who pursue Sharia Law through other methods do not fit his version of 'extremist.'

Salam al-Marayati – Obama Adviser, founder of Muslim Public Affairs Council and its current executive director. This is an article by the Militant Islam Monitor, on May 11, 2013, regarding al-Marayati:

"Salam Al Marayati, the director of the Muslim Public Affairs Council (MPAC), is scheduled to be on a panel at the upcoming National Homeland Security Conference in June in LA. The panel discussion is about "Public and Private" Partnerships. The program tracks "Interoperability, Information Sharing and Intelligence."

Arif Alikhan ,who was responsible for derailing the LAPD's plans to monitor activities within the Muslim community is also a speaker at the conference, He was appointed as assistant secretary for the Office of Policy Development in Barack Obama's Department of Homeland Security in 2009. According to 'Discover the Networks': MPAC has defended the use of terrorism and Al Marayati said on the radio on 9/11 that Israel could have been behind the attacks." In a November 1997 speech at the University of Pennsylvania, MPAC Co-Founder and Executive Director Salam Al-Marayati steadfastly refused to call Hezbollah a terrorist organization; he justified the existence of Hamas as a political entity and a provider of social programs and "educational operations" and he equated jihad with the sentiments of the American statesman Patrick Henry, whose "Give me liberty or give me death" declaration was, in Al-Marayati's view, "a way of looking at the term 'jihad' from an American perspective."

Al-Marayati will be participating in the NHS conference under the aegis of the Muslim American Homeland Security Congress an Islamist organization which attempts to prevent law enforcement scrutiny of Muslims, deny any Islamic connection to terrorism and hinder government efforts to educate people about the jihadist threat. Among the MAHSC listed board members is the Council on American Islamic Relations (CAIR) a Saudi funded front group for Hamas and an unindicted co-conspirator in the Holyland Foundation Hamas funding trial.

It should come as no surprise that Haroon Azar,the DHS Security Regional Director for Strategic Engagement, has worked with MPAC in the past. Haroon Azar took part in an MPAC teleconference aimed at portraying Muslims as victims of a non existent backlash after the Boston terrorist attacks.

Azar is also speaking on the same panel as Al Marayati at the upcoming NHS conference.

To have a documented Islamist leader of a major Muslim organization with known terrorist sympathies and Muslim Brotherhood ties on a panel at a NHS conference is further proof that our security apparatus is being manipulated by and adopting a jihadist perspective while doing everything it can to deny and obscure the threat which radical Islam poses to the security of the United States.

Imam Mohamed Magid – Obama's Sharia Czar, Islamic Society of North America. A PJ Media report on July 5, 2012 gave the following information about Mohamed Magid and his support for other radical Islamists:

"Mohamed Magid is the Obama administration's go-to guy for Muslim outreach and advise on international affairs and counterterrorism. He is a regular visitor to the White House (even when the administration wants to conceal it,) attends important administration speeches on the US Middle East policy at the State Department, he counsels the Department of Justice to criminalize defamation of Islam, he entertains the deputy national security adviser at his DC-area mosque, and he serves on the Department of Homeland Security's Countering Violent Extremism Working Group. He also advises the FBI and many other federal agencies. He has also been profiled by Time Magazine and the Huffington Post has even dubbed him "America's Imam." His ubiquitous presence across the Obama administration undoubtedly makes him the most influential and sought after Muslim authority in the country.

Imam Magid also serves as the president of the Islamic Society of North America (ISNA). In that capacity last weekend he presided over ISNA's "Diversity Forum" held in Dearborn (where Muslim residents were recently video recorded stoning Christian protestors). One of the speakers at the ISNA Diversity Forum was CAIR-Michigan executive director Dawud Walid. Imam Magid even gave a "diversity award" to Walid.

Walid, too, is popular with the Obama administration, taking two taxpayer financed trips overseas on behalf of the State Department. But just a little over a month ago Dawud Walid gave a sermon at the Islamic Organization of America (IONA) mosque in Warren, Michigan. As noted by an Investigative Project report issued just days after Walid's appearance, during the sermon he asked, "Who are those who incurred the wrath of Allah?" Answering his own question in Arabic, he replied, "They are the Jews, they are the Jews." Walid also took aim his imagined enemies, saying:

> "One of the greatest social ills facing American today is Islamophobia, and anti-Muslim bigotry. And if you trace the organizations and the main advocates and activists in Islamophobia in America, you will see that all those organizations are pro-Israeli occupation organizations and activists."

So not only are the Jews the cursed of Allah, but the Jews are also behind "Islamophobia" — reviving longtime Islamic blood libels. As the Investigative Project report goes on to note Walid has also taken to Twitter to correctly source and affirm Islamic authorities who called for killing Jews.

Imam Magid's endorsement of Walid's outspoken Jew-hatred raises some serious questions about who Obama is getting his advice from, but it does answer some questions about the inspiration for the Obama administration's ongoing "Islamophobia" witchhunt. But handing a "diversity award" to an unashamed Jew-hater doesn't make Dawud Walid a diversity hero. It does, however, say something about Obama's Shariah czar Mohamed Magid."

Eboo Patel – Advisory Council on Faith-Based Neighborhood Partnerships. Named by US News & World Report as one of America's Best Leaders of 2009, Eboo Patel is the founder and Executive Director of Interfaith Youth Core (IFYC), a Chicago-based institution building the global interfaith youth movement. Author of the award-winning book 'Acts of Faith: The Story of an American Muslim, the Struggle for the Soul of a Generation,' Eboo is also a regular contributor to the Washington Post, National Public Radio and CNN. He is a member of President Obama's Advisory Council of the White House Office of Faith Based and Neighborhood Partnerships, and holds a doctorate in the sociology of religion from Oxford University, where he studied on a Rhodes scholarship.

Although nothing specific has been reported to suggest he has the same Islamic inclinations as the others reported above, his inclusion in Obama's close administration must still be suspect. The idea of a 'global interfaith youth movement' itself could be suspect considering all the other aspects of Islam. Their ultimate goal is to turn everyone into Islamists. And, combine this approach with the global internet connection with all schools - they have the perfect vehicle to begin that insidious project.

Barack Obama and his administration have supported and promoted many of these Islamists under the guise of peace building and inclusion. But is that what's really happening? Let's analyze the organizations these Islamists openly support - especially the ISNA. Who or what is ISNA? The 'Investigative Project on Terrorism' answers this question:

"Established in 1981 by the Saudi-funded Muslim Students' Association of the U.S. and Canada (MSA), the Islamic Society of North America (ISNA) calls itself the largest Muslim organization on the continent. ISNA was created by MSA with the help of one of Palestanian Islamic Jihad's founding students, Sami Al-Irian. Another noteworthy founding member of ISNA was Mahboob Khan.

Today ISNA's annual conventions draw more attendees, usually over 30,000, more than any other Muslim gathering in the western hemisphere. ISNA's mission is to function as "an association of Muslim organizations and individuals that provides a common platform for presenting Islam, supporting Muslim communities, developing educational, social and outreach programs and fostering good relations with other religious communities, and civic and service organizations."

ISNA focuses heavily on providing Wahhabi theological indoctrination materials to a large percentage of the mosques in North America. Many of these mosques were recently built with Saudi money and are required, by their Saudi benefactors, to strictly follow the dictates of Wahhabi imams; an edict that affects the tone and content of the sermons given in the mosques, the selection of books and periodicals that may be read in mosque libraries or sold in mosque bookshops, and the policies governing the exclusion or suppression of dissenters from the congregations.

Through its affiliate, the North American Islamic Trust, a Saudi government-backed organization created to fund Islamist enterprises in North America, the Saudi-subsidized ISNA reportedly holds the mortgages on 50 to 80 percent of all mosques in the U.S. and Canada. Thus the organization can freely exercise ultimate authority over these houses of worship and their teachings.

Writes Kaukab Siddique, the editor of 'New Trend,' an Islamic periodical of extremist views that is nonetheless opposed to Wahhabi domination of American Islam: "ISNA controls most mosques in America and thus also controls who will speak at every Friday prayer, and which literature will be distributed there."

Islam scholar Stephen Schwartz describes ISNA as "one of the chief conduits through which the radical Saudi form of Islam passes into the United States."Adds Schwartz, "Our view is that the number of mosques under Wahhabi control actually totals at least 600 out of the official total of 1,200, while, as noted, Shia community leaders endorse the figure of 80 percent Wahhabi control. But we also offer a number of 6,000 mosques overall, including small and diverse congregations of many kinds."

According to Sufi leader Sheikh Muhammad Hisham Kabbani's testimony before a State Department Open Forum on January 7, 1999, extremists have taken over "more than 80 percent of the mosques in the United States. This means that the ideology of extremism has been spread to 80 percent of the Muslim population, mostly the youth and the new generation." Kabbani based his statement on his personal investigation of 114 American mosques. "Ninety of them," he said, "were mostly exposed, and I say exposed, to extreme or radical

ideology, based on their speeches, books and board members."
This is largely due to the efforts of ISNA.

According to terrorism expert Steven Emerson, ISNA "is a
radical group hiding under a false veneer of moderation;"
"convenes annual conferences where Islamist militants have
been given a platform to incite violence and promote hatred"
(for instance, al Qaeda supporter and PLO official Yusuf Al-
Qaradhawi was invited to speak at an ISNA conference); has
held fundraisers for terrorists (after Hamas leader Mousa
Marzook was arrested and eventually deported in 1997, ISNA
raised money for his defense); has condemned the U.S.
government's post-9/11 seizure of Hamas' and Palestinian
Islamic Jihad's financial assets; and publishes a bi-monthly
magazine, '*Islamic Horizons*,' that "often champions militant
Islamist doctrine."

Many more Islamic organizations, almost all in fact, that are
aimed at the one goal of a silent Jihad of changing America to
Sharia from within. They have all assigned themselves to that
charter - and Barack Obama is helping them achieve that goal.

The hard truth is: they could not accomplish that Jihadist goal
without Obama's help. Is he helping them destroy the United
States from sheer stupidity, or is he really part of that Jihad,
himself? Perhaps he really does understand what he's doing.
Or, is he perhaps guided in his relationship with Muslim
terrorists by a statement he made in 2007.

On November 21, 2007, then-candidate Obama said on New
Hampshire Public Radio that his Muslim experience would
make us safer:

"I truly believe that the day I'm inaugurated, not only the country looks at itself differently, but the world looks at America differently. If I'm reaching out to the Muslim world they understand that I've lived in a Muslim country and I may be a Christian, but I also understand their point of view.

My sister is half-Indonesian. I traveled there all the way through my college years. And so I'm intimately concerned with what happens in these countries and the cultures and perspective these folks have. And those are powerful tools for us to be able to reach out to the world. Then I think the world will have confidence that I am listening to them and that our future and our security is tied up with our ability to work with other countries in the world that will ultimately make us safer."
End of article.

The Muslim Brotherhood through the organization CAIR (Council on American-Islamic Relations) continues to push the Islamic agenda into every nook and cranny of American life. They are especially detrimental to and within our education systems. CAIR is always welcomed at the White House, and seems to have a close ear to the administration.

This is what Wikipedia introduces about CAIR:

"The Council on American–Islamic Relations (CAIR) is a Muslim civil liberties advocacy organization that deals with civil advocacy. It is headquartered on Capitol Hill in Washington, D.C., with regional offices nationwide.

Through media relations, lobbying, and education, CAIR presents an Islamic perspective on issues of importance to the American public, and seeks to empower the American Muslim community and encourage its social and political activism.

Annual banquets, through which CAIR raises the majority of its funds, are attended by American politicians, statesmen, interfaith leaders, activists and media personalities. Critics of CAIR consider it to be pursuing an extreme Islamic agenda.

In 2007 the organization was named, along with 245 others, by U.S. Federal prosecutors in a list of unindicted co-conspirators and/or joint venturers in a Hamas funding case involving the Holy Land Foundation, which in 2009 caused the FBI to cease working with CAIR outside of criminal investigations due to its designation. CAIR was never charged with any crime, and it complained that the designation had tarnished its reputation. Following a motion from CAIR and other groups, a federal appeals court sealed the list on October 20, 2010, ruling the designation violated the group's rights and was the result of "simply an untested allegation of the Government, made in anticipation of a possible evidentiary dispute that never came to pass."

CAIR has been criticized numerous times by various officials and organizations. The organization was criticized as pursuing an extremist Islamist agenda, and putting out propaganda. It has been listed as a terrorist group by the United Arab Emirates.

CAIR's mission statement is "to enhance understanding of Islam, encourage dialogue, protect civil liberties, empower American Muslims, and build coalitions that promote justice and mutual understanding".

CAIR's literature describes the group as promoting understanding of Islam and protecting Muslim civil liberties. It has intervened on behalf of many American Muslims who claim discrimination, profiling, or harassment. Its stated core principles include supporting freedom of religion, protecting all

Americans' civil rights, and encouraging inter-faith dialogue. CAIR believes that "the active practice of Islam strengthens the social and religious fabric of our nation."

CAIR is a nonprofit 501(c)(3) organization with affiliates in 20 states (many of which manage multiple offices), and 33 chapters in the US. CAIR and its affiliates are managed by board members from 50 American cities, and combined employ more than 70 full-time staff, serving millions of American Muslims. CAIR annual reports are available to all members and donors, as well as internet users online. End of article.

Many CAIR and ISNA leaders and members are customarily invited to White House events, especially events related to religion. While at the same time, leaders and representatives from other religions are customarily ignored.

CAIR and other Muslim Brotherhood organizations are constantly probing and prodding to get their tentacles into every organization or group in America, especially education. There are too many incidents to list here, but a simple internet inquiry into 'Islam and Education' reveals too many incidents with too many negative results and abominations toward America and its citizens." End of article.

Is Obama delusional, or is he lost in la-la land? The radical Muslim terrorist goal is to destroy us and anyone else who is not or does not convert to Islam. Why does he think his relationship with them, or who he is, will change that dogma? It seems his policies are leaned more to helping the silent jihad infiltrate into our schools, as well as everywhere else, instead of establishing policies to help our schools educate our children and help them find a sense of self worth, so they might find personal success that will help the economy of America as well as helping them find happiness for themselves.

Does Obama not understand that the ultimate tenant of Islam, radical and non-radical, is to make every person 'remaining' on earth a Muslim? Or does he understand it and is part of that process? Why does he not focus more on American progress, America's future, and the feeling of self worth for every American?

His actions to invite those who threaten to destroy us and our way of life to 'our dinner table' should also raise other questions regarding the safety and security of our great nation. Perhaps one of those questions might be 'what is the basis of his ideologies that guide his actions and decisions to protect America.' Let's let Obama expose his own ideologies.

Obama's guiding ideologies:

This is a list of quotes reported by Joshua Riddle at youngcons.com. The list contains 20 quotes giving Obama's views on Islam and Christianity. According to Riddle, "This is a great list highlighting how radical President Obama is when it comes to Islam and Christianity."

20 Quotes By Barack Obama About Islam and Mohammed:

#1 "The future must not belong to those who slander the Prophet of Islam."

#2 "The sweetest sound I know is the Muslim call to prayer."

#3 "We will convey our deep appreciation for the Islamic faith, which has done so much over the centuries to shape the world — including in my own country."

#4 "As a student of history, I also know civilization's debt to Islam."

#5 "Islam has a proud tradition of tolerance."

#6 "Islam has always been part of America."

#7 "we will encourage more Americans to study in Muslim communities."

#8 "These rituals remind us of the principles that we hold in common, and Islam's role in advancing justice, progress, tolerance, and the dignity of all human beings."

#9 "America and Islam are not exclusive and need not be in competition. Instead, they overlap, and share common principles of justice and progress, tolerance and the dignity of all human beings."

#10 "I made clear that America is not – and never will be – at war with Islam."

#11 "Islam is not part of the problem in combating violent extremism – it is an important part of promoting peace."

#12 "So I have known Islam on three continents before coming to the region where it was first revealed."

#13 "In ancient times and in our times, Muslim communities have been at the forefront of innovation and education."

#14 "Throughout history, Islam has demonstrated through words and deeds the possibilities of religious tolerance and racial equality."

#15 "Ramadan is a celebration of a faith known for great diversity and racial equality."

#16 "The Holy Koran tells us, 'O mankind! We have created you male and a female; and we have made you into nations and tribes so that you may know one another.'"

#17 "I look forward to hosting an Iftar dinner celebrating Ramadan here at the White House later this week, and wish you a blessed month."

#18 "We've seen those results in generations of Muslim immigrants – farmers and factory workers, helping to lay the railroads and build our cities, the Muslim innovators who helped build some of our highest skyscrapers and who helped unlock the secrets of our universe."

#19 "That experience guides my conviction that partnership between America and Islam must be based on what Islam is, not what it isn't. And I consider it part of my responsibility as president of the United States to fight against negative stereotypes of Islam wherever they appear."

#20 "I also know that Islam has always been a part of America's story."

Do any of these quotes by Barack Hussein Obama show or infer any respect for American citizens or the United States? Absolutely not. They demonstrate only his love and respect for the Islamic world; the world that has a written and proclaimed agenda to destroy us.

Can you even imagine a leader, especially the president of the United States, quoting the historical European Crusades to justify deadly attacks by terrorists razing through the Middle East with their aim to destroy Christians - and us? Yes, President Barack Obama did just that.

Since his term of office is scheduled to expire soon, if that really happens, what policies will his successor continue or implement? Will his successor be a Democrat who continues to ignore the security of the United States in favor of appeasement to anyone coming into our great nation; or in their wild rush to make them citizens so they can keep Democrats in office forever? How many immigrants will actually be part of terrorist cells, allowed to vote in our great nation? Or will it be a Republican who has enough concern, courage, and confidence who will insure our nation's security is the first priority of the presidential office? This is the prime dictate and first objective of that highest office in the land.

Clearly, that has not been the prime commitment of the one who now occupies that critical position of President of the United States of America. What will be the objective of the one who next occupies that position? Will his or her first priority be to 'protect American citizens and the fabric of what makes us American?' Or, will it be to rush everyone to vote; illegal, dead, or terrorist, just to remain in political office?

This is a critical time in the lifeline of our nation. Are there enough true American citizens and patriots who will make that right decision when they step inside the voting both? Or, will there be so many real non-citizens voting that the Muslim Brotherhood will be closer to fulfilling their goal of 'Settlement?' This is not merely a social and political question it's also a religious and survival question. The Muslim Brotherhood tentacles are everywhere, perhaps even connected to Hillary Clinton.

Chapter 6
Hillary, Abedin, and Alinsky

This is an article published by Frank Gaffney, Jr. at centerforsecuritypolicy.org The title is 'Huma Abedin's Private Emails and the Muslim Brotherhood, dated March 6, 2015:

"Hillary Clinton's Emailgate scandal is becoming more problematic by the day. Turns out she exclusively used a private email account while personally prohibiting other State Department employees from doing the same.

One other State Department official evidently violated this policy: Her Deputy Chief of Staff, Huma Abedin. Ms. Abedin's emails are of particular interest insofar as Huma has extensive ties to the Muslim Brotherhood. That's the Islamist organization whose self-declared mission is "destroying Western civilization from within."

The indispensable investigative group, Judicial Watch, has filed suit in federal court for access to these emails. It remains to be seen if they are provided and, if so, what they reveal about these ladies' contacts with the Muslim Brotherhood – and their damage-control concerning revelations about Huma's connection to it."

Who is Huma Abedin? This information about her is from Wikipedia:

"Huma Mahmood Abedin is an American political staffer of Pakistani descent. She has been a long-time aide to Hillary Clinton; she was U.S. Secretary of State Clinton's Deputy Chief of Staff at the State Department and before that, traveling chief of staff and "body woman" during Clinton's campaign for the Democratic nomination in the 2008 presidential election. She is married to former Democratic Congressman Anthony Weiner.

Abedin was born in Kalamazoo, Michigan. When she was two years old, her family moved to Jeddah, Saudi Arabia. Both her parents were educators. Her Indian father, Syed Zainul Abedin, born in New Delhi, India on April 2, 1928, graduated from Aligarh Muslim University in 1947 with a masters in English literature and joined the department's faculty as a lecturer. He later received his Ph.D. from the University of Pennsylvania. He died in 1993. Her Pakistani mother, Saleha Mahmood Abedin, also received her Ph.D. from the University of Pennsylvania, and is currently an associate professor of sociology at Dar Al-Hekma College in Jeddah.

Abedin returned to the United States at 18 to attend George Washington University, where she earned a B.A. degree.

While a student at George Washington University, Abedin began working as an intern in the White House in 1996, assigned to then-First Lady Hillary Rodham Clinton. In 1998, she was an assistant editor of the Journal of Muslim Minority Affairs. She later worked as traveling chief of staff and "body woman" during Clinton's 2008 Democratic Presidential nomination campaign, and subsequently served as Deputy Chief of Staff under Clinton in the State Department. She is currently a director of the transition team that is helping Clinton return to private life, and works for the William Jefferson Clinton Foundation.

In 2010, Abedin was included in Time's "40 under 40", a list of a "new generation of civic leaders" and "rising stars of American politics". At a celebration before Abedin's wedding to Anthony Weiner, Clinton said in a speech, "I only have one daughter. But if I had a second daughter, it would [be] Huma." End of Wikipedia information.

It's strange that Bill Clinton would make such a comment, since he was the one who 'officiated' the wedding between Abedin and Anthony Weiner. Even the ceremony itself has raised many questions; such as what was the purpose for the marriage and who arranged it. According to normal Islamic rituals, Abedin was and still proclaims to be a Muslim; she could not marry a man not himself a Muslim - unless he converted to Islam. Weiner has never claimed himself a Muslim. According to Islam, if he didn't convert, then Abedin would be considered an 'apostate' and would be subject to the fate demanded of apostates. This situation creates another question; are they really married?

The only person identified as officiating the wedding ceremony was Bill Clinton. For their wedding to be official, according to Islam, an Islamic official would have had to perform the ceremony. As with so many other things surrounding the Clintons, these questions have never been answered. This continuing secrecy and avoidance of truth and honesty creates much greater questions: why all the secrecy, and what dangers are created to our nation by those unknown questions.

And some serious questions might be asked of the involvement of Hillary Clinton and her Muslim assistant, Abedin, regarding events throughout the world affecting our security during Clinton's tenure as Secretary of State. These are only a few of those questions regarding Abedin's role or influence which might have affected either head of that great attack on America:

1. Was she involved in the Benghazi murders and its coverup?

2. Was she influential in the Benghazi review board?

3. What influence does she have with closer Iranian relations?

4. Did her Muslim Brotherhood influence affect the ouster of Qaddafi, in Libya and Mubarrak, in Egypt?

5. Did she influence the State Department's dismissal of the threat of ISIS - when Obama declared it was only a JV threat?

6. Perhaps the most important question must be asked about Abedin's influence as a Muslim (and a questionable member of the Muslim Brotherhood-Sisterhood): was she influential in soliciting and acquiring the millions of dollars the Clinton's got for their foundation from Muslim Brotherhood countries of Saudi Arabia, Algeria, United Arab Emirates, Kuwait, and Qatar?

Is Abedin a member of the secretive Muslim Brotherhood? Information from an interview with Walid Shoebat helps answer this question. That interview in 2012 was reported by frontpagemag.com, (FP) and conducted by Jamie Glazov. The article is titled: 'The Dark Muslim Brotherhood World of Huma Abedin.' Walid Shoebat was introduced as a former PLO terrorist and Muslim Brotherhood activist who is the author of the new book, 'For God or For Tyranny.'

These are selected excerpts from that interview:

"FP: You were the first to break the news on Huma Abedin, Anthony Weiner's wife, being linked to her mother Saleha Abedin, who, as you have exposed, has ties to the Muslim Brotherhood. First, let me ask you: how credible are your sources?

Shoebat: Al-Liwa Al-Arabi (translated here) leaked an extensive list, which was partially published by Al-Jazeera and several other major Arab newspapers. The detailed list included Huma's mother, Saleha Abedin.

Another piece of the puzzle and what was common knowledge in the Arab world is that Huma Abedin has a brother named Hassan Abedin who sits in on the board of the Oxford Centre For Islamic Studies (OCIS) where Huma's brother is a fellow and partners with a number of Muslim Brotherhood members on the Board, including Al-Qaeda associate, Omar Naseef and the notorious Muslim Brotherhood leader Sheikh Youssef Qaradawi; both have been listed as OCIS Trustees. Naseef continues to serve as Board Chairman.

This becomes an issue since Huma sits in the U.S. State Department with eyes and ears to classified government secrets. Was Huma unaware of all this as she accompanied Hillary Clinton to the Dar El-Hekma women's college in Jedda-Saudi Arabia? Huma's mother is the co-founder and a Vice Dean at the college and an active missionary on issues regarding Muslim women and is considered by the Egyptian security services as a dangerous member of the Muslim Brotherhood.

FP: What would you say to those who would argue that the Sisterhood organization is a farce and that the Egyptian Al-Dostor broke the news but that there is nothing really to substantiate this case?

Shoebat: The "Women's Division" within the Muslim Brotherhood can be found at the Muslim Brotherhood's official website. Here is an excerpt of its goal translated from Arabic states:

"The Womens Organization's goal in accordance with the Muslim Brotherhood rules, is to gain and acquire a unified global perception in every nation in the world regarding the position of women, and the necessity of advocacy work at all levels in accordance to the message of the Brotherhood as written in Women in Muslim Society, and the rearing of women throughout the different stages of life."

Al-Dostor's article is confirmed by top experts in Egypt including the Arab Center for Studies, headed by researcher Abdul Rahim Ali. That with the Muslim Brotherhood's own official statement gives us a solid case that this clandestine group called The Sisterhood exists, very active and very influential. So influential that they succeeded in getting Hillary Clinton to speak alongside two of its members; Abedin and Suheir Qureshi were also listed as members by several major Arab sources.

Then we have the links, which shows damning evidence that this list was not created haphazardly. We did the research which we shall release shortly; so many of who are on the list are official members or wives/daughters of members ranging from spies, Nazi-style propagandists, Nazi affiliates from the Brotherhood's inception, Hijab advocates in Europe, and prominent conspiracy theory advocates with a span of influence over several international organizations from the United Nations to women advocacy groups worldwide.

FP: Can you please give us an example of one case?

Shoebat: I will give a taste of one case.

Keep in mind the Muslim Brotherhood is Egyptian and so is Huma's heritage. The Sisterhood List includes wives/daughters of top Brotherhood leaders mostly from Egypt. We have Najla Ali Mahmoud, the wife of Mohammed Aidalmrsi, who is a member of the Guidance Bureau of the Muslim Brotherhood and the current leader of the Justice and Freedom Party, (the new name for the Muslim Brotherhood). No one can deny his affiliation and his wife is definitely following his footsteps.

FP: Other than Huma Abedin, has there ever been any member of the Muslim Brotherhood or a prominent Islamist who will not openly denounce a "daughter" or "sister" that married a non-Muslim Jewish male?

Shoebat: It is extremely rare to have Muslim women marry non-Muslims, much less to have conservative Muslims look the other way, unless Huma has a "higher calling" and a unique exception was made for her, since she is an ear into top U.S. sensitive information, or Anthony Weiner has converted to Islam or even both.

There is no other way to answer this unless Huma comes up with an astonishing revelation. The highest authority in Islamic Sharia Faculty in Kuwait has deemed Huma's marriage to a male Jew as null and void, yet no word from her family or the Muslim Brotherhood to affirm the Isamic Sharia Faculty?

Huma—keep in mind—was in contact with her mother when she visited Dar Al-Hikma University with Hillary Clinton. Huma's dress code alone would be a problem for her mother, much less her unequally yoked marriage to a male Jew.

Huma's marriage should be a stab in the heart to religious Muslims. She comes from a prominent family. It's like saying a nun stabbed the Pope in the heart, yet the Vatican issues no condemnation and instead was sympathetic to the woman for simply being a woman. Something would be very fishy. Huma's Muslim Brotherhood connected family still has contacts, admiration and appreciation for her." End of interview article.

What is the conclusion from these revelations that the highest offices of our government invite our enemy (or those who might be suspected of being associated with those who threaten to destroy us) into those high positions of trust and leadership? It means perhaps their ability to make important decisions should be questioned or challenged.

Hillary Clinton's actions to invite those who threaten to destroy us and our way of life to 'our dinner table' should also raise other questions regarding the safety and security of our great nation. Perhaps one of those questions might be 'what is the basis of her ideologies that guide her actions regarding the safety and security of the United States. Let's let Hillary Clinton expose her own ideologies.

Hillary Clinton's guiding ideology:

By now, certainly everyone (who has an ear) is aware of all Hillary's lies and deceptions. There are too many to list here, but two stand out the most. They are her claim that a video caused the deaths of four Americans in Benghazi, including Ambassador Chris Stevens, and her close association with Saul Alinsky.

In her position as head of the State Department she knew the truth, but instead of the truth she tried to deceive us. Her most recent act of deception was her use of the private email account, and server, for official government business - exposing all that information to being hacked and extracted by our enemies. Her ideology of deception is unquestionable. Huma Abedin also had access to all that information.

Another serious question must also be explored about her association and political influence from her 'friend,' yes friend, named Saul Alinsky. Saul Alinsky was a left-wing organizer whose goal, according to his writings, was to destroy the 'status-quo' of the United States. His two popular books were: 'Rules for Radicals' and 'Reveille for Radicals.'

Hillary Clinton was associated with Alinsky in 1968-1969, and even wrote her college thesis at Wellesley college in 1968 about his theories. Was she close to and a friend of Alinsky? Read part of a letter she sent to him in 1971:

"Dear Saul, when is that new book coming out, or has it come and I somehow missed the fulfillment of Revelation? (Referring to Rules for Radicals)

I have just had my one-thousandth conversation about Reveille and need some new material to throw at people.

The more I've seen of places like Yale Law School and the people who haunt them, the more convinced I am that we have the serious business and joy of much work ahead—if the commitment to a free and open society is ever going to mean more than eloquence and frustration.

If I never thanked you for the encouraging words of last spring in the midst of the Yale-Cambodia madness, I do so now.

I am living in Berkeley and working in Oakland for the summer and would love to see you. Let me know if there is any chance of our getting together." The letters can be read at this site:

http://freebeacon.com/politics/the-hillary-letters/

What was Saul Alinsky's Plan? How did it influence Hillary Clinton's ideology?

Who is Saul Alinsky and what were his plans for guiding radicals toward a social revolution in America? He was a social radical who wrote two books to promote social revolution. Hillary Clinton had several meetings with him to exchange information in her early years. Barack Obama not only endorsed these rules written by Alinsky, he also taught Alinsky's tactics while he was a 'community organizer.' The following information explains further.

Alinsky's important books are: 'Rules for Radicals' and 'Reveille for Radicals.' In the books he explains how to create a social state. According to him there are eight levels of control that must be obtained before you are able to create a social state. The first is the most important.

1. **Healthcare**: Alinsky wrote, "Control healthcare and you control the people.' This is the first attack on the "establishment."

Isn't it ironic this was also Obama's first and most critical action when he became president. Isn't it also ironic that during her husband's administration, Hillary Clinton tried to have a healthcare law passed that would have served the same purpose - to control the people. Finally, enough legislators were convinced through many tactics, to vote for his healthcare bill. Now, his Affordable Care Act, also known as Obamacare, will soon cripple our nation financially.

2. **Poverty**: "Increase the poverty level as high as possible, poor people are easier to control and will not fight back if you are providing everything for them to live."

Just look how Obama has created a broader welfare state; welfare, food stamps, special programs to distribute the wealth. There are twice as many people getting food stamps now as when he came into office. The median earnings for American citizens have also gone down $2000 since he became president.

3. **Debt**: "Increase the debt to an unsustainable level. That way you are able to increase taxes, and this will produce more poverty."

Obama has increased the national debt faster and greater than any president ever; even faster than all the previous presidents combined. It's now over 18 trillion dollars - and growing. He doesn't even discuss the national debt or what to do about it. He occasionally mentions 'budget deficit' which is not the same as the national debt. He consistently and strongly attempts to increase taxes - especially on wealthy people and corporations. He has never discussed cutting the budget at any source - only spending more to give everyone their 'fair share.' Hillary Clinton shares this spending and government control concept with her ideas in 'It Takes A Village.' In other words she believes individuals are incapable of thinking and doing for themselves.

4. Gun Control: "Remove the ability to defend themselves from the government. That way you are able to create a police state."

The president has made no secret of his interest in enacting more stringent gun control across the board in America. While he smiles and tries to cloak his goals in the guise of a "reasonable approach to gun control", he quietly and behind the scenes schemes with his Attorney General Eric Holder to use whatever tactics they can to achieve as much as they can, with little regard for what the majority of the American people want. Hillary Clinton supports his gun policies, in accordance with her devotion to Alinsky's rules and ideas. Is this a reasonable approach toward weapons and protection? Even the Bible proposes we not be defenseless in the name of 'safety and protection.'

First Thessalonians, Chapter 5, Verses 2-3 states, "For yourselves know perfectly that the day of the Lord so cometh as a thief in the night. 3, For when they shall say, Peace and safety; then sudden destruction cometh upon them, as travail upon a woman with child; and they shall not escape."

Any action that reduces gun ownership by American citizens will put our nation at great risk. Not only does the Bible warn us; it's also just common sense not to voluntarily become totally defenseless against harm in any manner. Hillary has consistently expressed her strong support of Alinsky's radical policies.

5. **Welfare**: "Take control of every aspect of their lives."

This is an article Thenewamerican.com, submitted by Alex Newman on 10 Jan. 2012. It's only one article that explains the growing welfare state in America since Obama became president:

"Fifty years ago this week, President Lyndon Johnson announced the "War on Poverty" during his first State of the Union speech. Under the Obama administration, however — five decades, countless unconstitutional federal welfare programs, and more than $20 trillion later — poverty levels remain largely unchanged even based on official numbers, and dependence on government has reached unprecedented new heights.

In reality, Americans' economic fate is far worse than even bogus government statistics would suggest. Even more troubling is that analysts say the trends look set to accelerate as Washington, D.C., intensifies its failed efforts to supposedly achieve "victory" in the "war" while the Federal Reserve conjures ever greater quantities of currency into existence.

Since Obama took office, 13 million more Americans have become dependent on food stamps, with the numbers now hitting a record 47 million — about a third more than when he was sworn in. In 2007, there were 26 million recipients. Spending on the scheme has more than doubled just since 2008.

The explosion of the program, along with other welfare schemes, has resulted in countless commentators and critics labeling Obama "the Food Stamp President."

This is one of Alinsky's rules. Does anyone suggest Hillary Clinton would ignore it?

6. **Education**: "Take control of what people read and listen to – take control of what children learn in school."

What is Hillary Clinton's answer to this rule? 'It Takes A Village."

7. **Religion**: "Remove the belief in their God from the Government and schools."

This has largely already been accomplished. Following Alinsky's ideas, but even worse; Christianity has been pushed aside to make room for Islam in government and schools. Is there any reason to believe Hillary Clinton would change these policies to replace Christianity with Islam? She has expressed deep support for his 'rules.'

8. **Class Warfare**: "Divide the people into the wealthy and the poor. This will cause more discontent and it will be easier to take (Tax) the wealthy with the support of the poor."

Does anyone doubt that Obama has not already further separated the rich and the poor in our country? At every opportunity and at every event and at every speech he makes he rarely misses the opportunity to speak of the 'greedy rich people' and their abuse and disregard of the less fortunate; denying them their 'fair share.' Hillary Clinton has repeatedly echoed Obama's 'greedy rich people' mantra - while she collects millions of dollars from leaders and other individuals across the world.

Her Worshipers.

What's amazing about Hillary Clinton? Millions of beguiled innocent followers and worshipers will support her no matter what she does or says. In the words of Karl Marx, Friedrich Engels, and Joseph Stalin they are 'Useful Idiots' and 'Useful Innocents.' In George Orwell's book '1984' he describes them as 'Proles,' as related to the proletariat who were enticed to destroy Russia by leaders of the Bolshevik Revolution. Mother Russia was destroyed.

What will happen to the United States when innocent Proles are encouraged to rise and destroy our great nation. Saul Alinsky's only aim with his books and rhetoric was to destroy the 'Status-Quo' not to replace it with something better; just destroy it. How much of his ideology remains with Hillary Clinton?

Chapter 7
Islam and Sharia

Finally, what is the greatest threat from the Islamic two-headed beast? Is it from the first and most vicious head of the attack - terrorism? Although many atrocities might be committed by this maniacal viciousness, the attacks themselves wouldn't affect the safety and security of our nation. It would be a harsh and deadly act upon many unsuspecting and innocent individuals, but our nation would survive; perhaps not with the real freedom we expect as Americans; but we would survive as a nation. Unfortunately, in any military war there are always many innocent victims.

The real victim from these attacks would be our freedom; that freedom allowed under our great Constitution. It allows us to do things and say things and to own things in a way that can't even be imagined in many countries, especially those countries whose citizens are bound by Islamic laws. At the moment we are free; free individuals and free people. Now we have no fear of daily life; that's what would be taken from us by terrorist attacks upon our soil. It would take only a few acts of terror to embolden that fear. That fear would restrict our movements and bind our words.

We would no longer be real 'Americans' as we now understand the definition of an American. But, even under this fear, we would still judge ourselves and our neighbors by a moral code of humanity.

So, what is the greatest Islamic threat to our nation and others? The most brazen threat is already showing itself throughout the Mideast and Africa. The radical Islamists show no mercy, no human decency, or no respect for any mankind as they mercilessly slaughter thousands of innocent people within the lands into which they continue to flow. They 'are drunken with the blood of martyrs of Jesus' as they flow like an amoeba running amuck over every land they touch.

According to their dogmatic rhetoric they are the 'Soldiers of Allah' enforcing his will. Their plan is to make everyone in their wake a Muslim, worshiping Allah and to enforce Sharia law. But, what is this Sharia law they are so desperate to force upon everyone? This list below offered by billionbibles.org summarizes major parts.

According to the Sharia law:

"Theft is punishable by amputation of the right hand.

Criticizing or denying any part of the Quran is punishable by death.

Criticizing or denying Muhammad is a prophet is punishable by death.

Criticizing or denying Allah, the moon god of Islam, is punishable by death.(This moon god is discussed below.)

A Muslim who becomes a non-Muslim is punishable by death.

A non-Muslim who leads a Muslim away from Islam is punishable by death.

A non-Muslim man who marries a Muslim woman is punishable by death.

A man can marry an infant girl and consummate the marriage when she is 9 years old.

Girls' clitoris should be cut (per Muhammad's words in Book 41, Kitab Al-Adab, Hadith 5251).

A woman can have 1 husband, but a man can have up to 4 wives; Muhammad can have more.

A man can unilaterally divorce his wife but a woman needs her husband's consent to divorce.

A man can beat his wife for insubordination.

Testimonies of four male witnesses are required to prove rape against a woman.

A woman who has been raped cannot testify in court against her rapist(s).

A woman's testimony in court, allowed only in property cases, carries half the weight of a man's.

A female heir inherits half of what a male heir inherits.

A woman cannot drive a car, as it leads to fitnah (upheaval).

A woman cannot speak alone to a man who is not her husband or relative.

Meat to be eaten must come from animals that have been sacrificed to Allah - i.e., be Halal.

Muslims should engage in Taqiyya and lie to non-Muslims to advance Islam. Lying, falsehoods, and deceptions are encouraged if the aim is to protect Islam and to spread its influence." There are more similar stringent rules in Sharia law.

Do influential people who understand what Sharia law really is support the implementation of Sharia in America? Consider what Representative Maxine Waters (D-CA) said in 2012 when she spoke at an Islamic Society of Orange County town hall meeting on the issue of the Constitution and Sharia law:

"Over the last year, and due to the focus of House Republicans on so-called 'Muslim radicalization,' we have seen politicians and pundits attacking the Islamic faith as a security threat to the United States. Across the country, these people are exploiting fear and trying to convince state legislatures that the state adoption of Sharia tenants is the strategy extremists are using to transform the United States into an Islamic country."

Many leaders in our nation, some at the highest levels, share this same view as Maxine Waters, that there are too many attacks against Islam. Perhaps she and those others don't understand; it's not attacks against Islam, it's a defense against Islam attacking America and the freedoms our Constitution allows us.

In summary, two things seem very clear from this list of Sharia law. First, it clearly demonstrates a hatred for, and encourages abuse of women, girls, and female babies. There are no restrictions against men that are even comparable to those horrors imposed on females, in that law. One could even imagine a sex lust was involved.

That might even be further supported by the concept of a martyr getting 72 virgins at the completion of his or her martyr mission. (Would a female martyr get those same 72 virgins? And, what would happen? Without a physical body present, would those 72 virgins be there just to view as trophies - or what?)

What reasonable person could even have conceived of such an idea! These atrocities are so heinous one must ask, 'what is the basis for this horror?' One might also reasonably ask, 'Is it a religion leading to heavenly salvation; or is it thuggery guided by a lust for raw power by individuals and by a group?' To learn more, let's explore the beginnings of Islam. Why is the crescent moon Islam's symbol?

The foundation of Islam:

Although Muslims argue that their god Allah is connected to the Christian god in the Bible, many historians suggest that's not the case at all. There's much speculation that Islam's god, Allah, is actually an interpretation of an ancient pagan moon god. One source is billionbibles.org, which suggests the crescent moon used in Islamic symbolism actually comes from an older version of the moon god, which was one of over two hundred gods worshiped in pagan times before the rise of Islam in Mecca. The following information is from billionbibles.org in an article titled, 'Allah Moon God.'

"Is Allah the God of the Bible, or is Allah the moon god of ancient pagan Arabia?

While "Allah" could refer to God literally, the Allah of Islam is the moon god of ancient pagan Arabia.

The Arabic word for "god" is "ilah", while "al" is the Arabic for "the". Therefore, "Allah" combines "al" with "ilah" and removes the "i", to literally means, "the god".

But much like "YHWH/Yahweh/Jehovah" is the personal name of the God of the Bible, "Allah" was also the personal name given to the moon god, the highest of the 360 pagan idols worshipped in Mecca, Muhammad's home town.

What evidence is there that Islam's "Allah" is the pagan moon god of ancient Mecca?

Consider what the pagan Arabians did to worship their moon god, Allah; they prayed while bowing towards K'abah, the "house of Allah" in Mecca that houses a meteorite - a stone from space - several times a day, visited it once a year, and walked around it several times during their visit.

Kabah Hajj - To worship their Allah today:

• Muslims pray bowing towards the K'abah in Mecca five times a day.

• About two million Muslims visit Mecca every year and walk around the K'abah (the black cube, which is 40 feet tall, on the right).

• The Muslim "holy" month of Ramadan starts at the sighting of a new crescent moon.

• Perched atop churches across the world is the cross, the symbol of the sacrifice made by our God. Perched atop mosques across the world is the crescent moon, the symbol of Allah whom Muhammad chose as the god of Islam.

When confronted with the details above, Muslims typically re-assert that "Allah" still means "al" + "ilah" - i.e., "the" + "god" - and is same as the God of the Bible, not the moon god of pagan Mecca. They even point out that Arabic Christian Bibles uses "Allah" to refer to God.

The "Allah" in the current Arabic Christian Bibles is literally "the God" and does refer to the God of the Bible. Advise Muslims that if this is really the "Allah" they are worshipping, then they should stop bowing down toward a meteorite five times a day and the crescent moon should neither start their "holy" month of Ramadan nor top their mosques. If the Allah they are worshipping is the God of the Bible, then they should worship Him as the Bible instructs." End of article.

This is more information about the black stone, the meteorite toward which Muslims pray five times a day. It's published by Historicalmysteries.com and submitted by Shelly Barclay in 2011. The article is titled, The Black Stone of Kaaba:

"Every day, five times a day, Muslims across the globe face Mecca and pray. When they face Mecca, it is not Mecca that they are truly facing, it is a cube-shaped building known as the Ka'aba or simply Kaaba. This building is also known as Baitullah or "The House of Allah." On the east corner of this revered building, there is a cornerstone known as the Black

Stone of the Ka'aba. It is steeped in mystery, legend and speculation.

The Ka'aba resides in Makka or Mecca, Saudi Arabia. It stands in the relative center of the Al-Haram Mosque, where millions of Muslims flock every year to see this building and walk around it seven times. Most of the year, it is covered in black cloth. Beneath the black cloth is a stone building that may date back as far as 2030 B.C.E. Each side of the cube measures about 60 ft. across. There is a gold door in the southeast side. Inside, there is a polished marble floor and three pillars.

Muslims believe that Allah himself ordered that the Ka'aba be constructed. The story is that Abraham built the mosque with his oldest son, Ishmael. The building is said to be the likeness of Allah's home in heaven. It is supposedly the oldest mosque on Earth. Historians believe it was once used by pagans, before Islam came into being. Likewise, the Black Stone is said to have been placed there and used by pagans, who were worshipful of such natural things. Islam forbids idolatry, so the Black Stone is not revered by them. They tell a completely different story about what the rock is and why it is so important.

There are various, slightly different, versions of the following story regarding the significance and origin of the Kaaba Black Stone. All are similar. When Adam was banished from Paradise or The Garden of Eden, he was filled with sin. The Black Stone was given to Adam to erase him of this sin and give him entrance into heaven. It is said to be from Heaven. At the time it belonged to Adam, it was white. Now, it is black because it has absorbed so much sin.

Muslims believe that the prophet Mohammad kissed the Black Stone and so, they kiss the Black Stone, if it is possible, during their obligatory, at least once a lifetime, trip to Ka'aba. If they are unable to kiss the stone, they point to it every time they pass on their seven-circle journey around the Ka'aba. This is a story steeped in religion and important religious figures. Therefore, the Black Stone has great importance as being linked to Allah, Adam and Muhammad. However, those outside of the Muslim faith have little to go by.

The Black Stone of the Ka'aba has been described as somewhere around 2 ft. in length. It is broken into roughly seven pieces, which are held together in a silver frame. The surface is certainly a blackish color, but there is some speculation that the color derives from all of the hands and mouths that have touched it, as well as the oils with which it is anointed. Not knowing the true color for sure makes it difficult to say just what it is. There is also a problem with getting a sample. Taking a sample would be extremely disrespectful. It might even be dangerous. There are stories about people being killed for messing around with the stone and the Ka'aba.

Thus far, speculation about the Kaaba Black Stone regard it being old, of course, and placed there by pagans. Those interested have postulated that the stone may be glass, agate or meteorite. It may also be glass from a meteorite. It is obviously brittle or it has been damaged by something very strong, which is certainly possible, considering it has been stolen and in the midst of a war in its history. Evidence pointing to any of these theories is slim, though the meteorite theory is the most popular. In the end, the stone holds much less importance to non-Muslims, so the mystery of its origins will have to be left to myth and legend for now. End of article.

Regarding the question of the two religions, Islam and Christianity, the questions of source and clarity must be considered if one is truly concerned about afterlife and salvation. Of course, Atheists don't have this consideration. They think life is so simple; you just live it, then you die, your body turns to dust, and that's the end of it.

Perhaps the strong desire and hope that's not the end of it; that life is so precious it must go on in some form is the basis of religion and salvation. The great fault line between these two religions is the method and the source to reach that everlasting salvation, that trip through eternity. The sources to those salvations are totally opposite.

In Islam, one has no choice. The source is to be a Muslim at birth and never abandon that source, or to become a Muslim by acceptance, coercion, or threat of death. It's a religion forced from a power base; as was Muhammed, an ancient warrior. He didn't sacrifice for his followers, he commanded them to be what they were to become. Muslims claim to follow a religion of 'peace.' Has anything of 'peace' ever been described in Islamic history? Nothing other than words; nothing in their deeds. Islam is a religion of force and coercion, if it's truly a religion at all.

On the other hand, Christianity is based on acceptance. It's impossible to convert one to Christianity by force or intimidation. One might say or agree to become a Christian when forced to say those words, but inside in their own hearts they know if they are a Christian or not. It's the inside event that determines whether one is a Christian and has accepted the love of that guiding Father to earn salvation in the afterlife. Christians believe Jesus was sent to earth to set an example and to show the way to salvation. He didn't come to earth with a sword and shield to slay all non-believers. He demonstrated with His life that it's a deep personal choice. Christianity is a religion of love, compassion, and acceptance.

The two-headed beast identified.

Yes, there clearly is a two-headed Islamic beast; and he's described and identified in the Bible; centuries before he appeared to create havoc and devastation upon the earth. The Apostle John described this beast with two heads in the Book of Revelation. The religion, Islam, is described in Chapter 17, Verses 3 through 6 as a 'woman' riding a scarlet colored beast. Verse 5 says she is the mother of harlots and abominations of the earth. Verse 6 says she will be drunken with the blood of the martyrs of Jesus. The beast encompasses that total religion.

Verse 5 identifies a harlot, a whore, separate from the religion filled with 'abominations.' That whore 'terrorists', will be drunken with the blood of the saints and the martyrs of Jesus. The terror of this whore is identified more in the section of the Bible known commonly to many as 'the mark of the beast.'

Another beast - the world leader: the Antichrist

Chapter 13 describes a first beast and a second beast. The second beast supports the first beast and has an image built for him. Then, Verse 15 states, "And he had power to give life unto the image of the beast, that the beast should both speak and cause that as many as would not worship the image of the beast should be killed." The terrorists are already doing this with their endless atrocities of murder and beheadings throughout the world.

Perhaps it might be negligent to end this message without including the next three verses in Chapter 13: 16, "And he causeth all, both small and great, rich and poor, free and bond, to receive a mark in their right hand, or in their foreheads;" (Could this mean a number that one would remember - in their foreheads - or a card they would present in their right hands?)

Verse 17, "And that no man might buy or sell, save he that had the mark, or the name of the beast, or the number of his name." (Could this mean a master computer that would have information about every person on earth; and that any transactions would be authorized and recorded on this computer? Consider the new NSA Security Center nearing completion in Bluffdale, Utah. It will have the capability to record everything about every person on earth for the next twenty years.)

Verse 18, "Here is wisdom. Let him that hath understanding count the number of the beast; for it is the number of a man; and his number is Six hundred threescore and six(666)." Two things here are very interesting. First the statement simply says to count; not interpret. Counting 6+6+6 equals 18. The second amazing thing is that this information is included where; in Verse **18**. It's a checkpoint saying to count 18. Is this not a good clue to count the number of letters in the beast's name? His full name should contain 18 letters.

Is it the name he was given or is it the name he chose for himself? Two snakes coiled together on a ring and worn proudly should help answer this long and mysterious question.

Conclusion

Until one understands that final moment of physical life he or she doesn't really understand the full concept of the afterlife and salvation. This presents the distinction between the reality of religion and belief by force and intimidation, or religion by understanding and acceptance. At that moment, at that crossover time, the difference is perfectly exposed; there's a total understanding. It's where the concept of 'believers being part of God' makes perfect sense.

Standing there before the 'Pearly Gates' with familiarity all around, one's spirit pauses before crossing over. While understanding that he or she is part of 'Godliness' that spirit asks the question only he or she can answer. That question is: 'Have I lived my life as was the purpose for my being placed on earth; or did I abandon that purpose somewhere along the way; am I worthy to cross over?' The answer, that right to cross over, doesn't come quick or easy.

Surprisingly, there is no loud voice from Saint Peter or God that says yes or no. The shock is that the spirit standing at the crossover point is part of the Spirit of God; and must answer that question himself or herself. And, before that spirit can answer there's total recall of every event in that person's life. It happens in the blink of an eye. That individual, the spirit of that person, must answer that question himself or herself. God is not a separate entity; He's part of the total Spirit included in every accepting individual.

After I answered that question, 'Yes,' I then had a choice to cross over or to return, obviously because my physical body was not damaged. I chose to return. Suddenly there was a big thump in my chest as I opened my eyes in the darkness of sleep and tried to breath; I first had to unwrap the sheet wound tightly around my neck. A large new cast had just been placed on my leg after knee surgery. The cast had not allowed the sheet to move with my body as I rolled over in my sleep. My first few deep breaths returning me to full life were difficult. It took a few minutes for my lungs to stop struggling for more oxygen.

Since that time I've been filled with total happiness that no one can destroy. For a while after that experience my greatest fear was that I might have that experience again and choose not to return. It was a wonderful and glorious place in which to enter. I felt I was given the choice to return for a purpose. I'm trying to fulfill that perceived purpose.

This is blog I recently posted at my blog site on Authorsden.com. I should repeat it here, since it concerns religion and salvation - and the 'end of times.'

Revelation offers hope - not despair

I've been reading the Book of Revelation fervently for several months; perhaps as much as two years, trying to interpret some of the meanings of those highly coded words and sentences. My last few blogs have been from the results of some of that interpretation.

While reading more as the source for my upcoming book, 'The Seven Spirits,' I was surprised to interpret - in my own way - that the Book of Revelation does not describe the end of the world - as many readers fear. It describes some horrible times resulting from plagues, wars, and natural disasters wherein many people will be killed. It also describes a religious war in which that religion led by a 'beast' representing a 'strange' god is finally defeated.

(Daniel 11: 39, "Thus shall he do in the most strong holds with a strange god whom he shall acknowledge and increase with glory; and he shall cause them to rule over many, and shall divide the land for gain.")

The location of that final battle is given in Revelation 16:14-16, which indicates Armageddon. The word 'Armageddon' is derived from Meggido, which is an ancient site on the edge of Jezreel Valley. Jezreel is also mentioned elsewhere in the Bible and was the location of many ancient battles. Chapter 19: 11-21 explains the result of that battle won by those 'upon white horses.'

When will this great battle occur? Perhaps Second Thessalonians, Chapter 2: 6-8, gives a clue: "And now ye know what withholdeth that he might be revealed in his time. For the mystery of iniquity doth already work; only he who now letteth will let, until he be taken out of the way, And then shall that Wicked be revealed, whom the Lord shall consume with the spirit of his mouth,"

Perhaps when the 'restrainer' is removed; when the United States no longer protects Israel, Israel will be attacked; 'when he who now letteth will let.'   Today, the respect for

Christianity, and the protection of Israel moves further away. Is this another signal that the 'end times' moves closer?

After that great battle, some of the last verses describe a new story. It seems many people do not read through to those last verses.

Chapter 21, Verse 24 reads, "And the nations of them which are saved shall walk in the light of it: (referring to the new city of Jerusalem) and the kings of the earth do bring their glory and honour into it." Glory and Honor are two of the seven Spirits. "And the nations of them which are saved" suggests our physical world as we know it will continue.

Chapter 22, Verse 2, "...was the tree of life, which bare twelve manner of fruits, and yielded her fruit every month: and the leaves of the tree were for the healing of the nations." Verse 4 adds, "And they that see his face; and his name shall be in their foreheads." Verse 12 warns, "And, behold, I come quickly; and my reward is with me, to give every man according to his work shall be." Note again that nations still exist, but must be healed. This confirms that our physical world will still exist for mankind to enjoy even greater.

Perhaps the physical world will continue to exist even after the great tribulation and after the Battle of Armageddon, and after God sits on His throne in His New Jerusalem. There is hope for humanity.

In the end, according to the last verses in the Bible, it will be a better world without the presence of that strange god, that two-headed beast, to wreak evil upon the earth. Everyone will live in the Light of those Seven Spirits of God: Power, Strength,

Riches, Blessings, Wisdom, Honor, and Glory. The two-headed beast will no longer exist.

God bless America and all those in the Spirit.

About the Author

Will Clark's author experiences began by writing inspection and evaluation reports in the U.S. Air Force. He is a retired Air Force officer and a Vietnam veteran, serving in Saigon from 1966 to 1967. His other overseas assignments include Misawa, Japan and Ankara, Turkey.

In 1995, he authored a book, *How to Learn*, as a county-wide study skills project to encourage students to improve their grades in DeSoto County, Mississippi. Education supporters printed and distributed four thousand copies. He also wrote a weekly education column for a local newspaper, *The Desoto County Tribune,* the following school year.

His next published book was *School Bells and Broken Tales*, a parody of nursery rhyme characters, also a motivation and education book for children. His other books include *Shades of Retribution,* a historical novel, and *Simply Success,* a motivation guide for students and employees.

His action novels include a trilogy based on Atlantis and crystals. The first book is titled: *The Atlantis Crystal.* The second book is titled: *She Waits In Atlantis.* The third is: *Return to Atlantis.* This trilogy is based on his travels while assigned to Turkey, site of the ancient city of Troy.

His previous political action novel, *666: Mark of the Beast*, is a sequel to another political action novel, *America 20XX: The New World Order.*

Clark and his wife, Marie, live in Diamondhead, Mississippi, where they play golf with many friends.

Things We Must Never Forget
Until We Know All the Answers

Benghazi

Why were four Americans killed?
Where was Hillary Clinton while it was happening?
Where was Barack Obama while it was happening?
Why did they lie and blame the event on a video?
Why were rescuers on 'stand by' told to 'stand down?'

Fast and Furious

Who authorized the operation?
Why did the operation continue after weapons were lost?
Why did the procedure have no procedure?
Why weren't tracking devices used?

The IRS Scandal

What was the highest level involved?
Who initiated it?
Why hasn't anyone been fired or reprimanded?
What dangers could be unleashed by this organization?

Greatest Quotes
of Our Time

Michelle Obama
February 18, 2008
"For the first time in my adult life I am proud of my country."
(Age 44)

Barack Obama
March 9, 2008
"We are no longer a Christian nation - at least not just."

September 25, 2012
Remarks to the UN General Assembly
"The future must not belong to those who slander Islam."

Nancy Pelosi
March 9, 2010
"We have to pass the bill so that you can find out what is in it."

Hillary Clinton
January 23, 2013
"What difference, at this point, does it make?"

December 3, 2014
"...showing respect even for one's enemies, trying to understand and insofar as psychologically possible, empathize with their perspective and point of view."

Other Books by the Author

Novels:
Shades of Retribution
The Atlantis Crystal
She Waits in Atlantis
Return to Atlantis
America 20XX: The New World Order
666: Mark of the Beast
Death Drones: 2025

Children's Books:
Forest Trails and Fairy Tales
Wishing Wells and Broken Tales
Student Study Skills
American Heroes: Students Who Learn

Non-Fiction:
Simply Success
The Education Jungle
How to Learn
The Day America Died
Obama's Ring: The Seat of Satan
Managing Without Conflict
The Peer Pressure Monster
The War on Christians
Who is the Antichrist
The War on Christians
The Seven Spirits
Obama, Hillary, Saul Alinsky and their Useful Idiots
Armed Patroits

www.ingramcontent.com/pod-product-compliance
Lightning Source LLC
Chambersburg PA
CBHW070924290526
45795CB00001B/410